AWKWARD SITUATIONS
FOR MEN

Danny Wallace

AWKWARD SITUATIONS FOR MEN

EBURY
PRESS

3 5 7 9 10 8 6 4 2

First published in 2010 by Ebury Press, an imprint of Ebury Publishing
A Random House Group company

The Random House Group Limited Reg. No. 954009

Addresses for companies within the Random House Group can be found at
www.randomhouse.co.uk

A CIP catalogue record for this book is available from the British Library

The Random House Group Limited supports The Forest Stewardship
Council (FSC), the leading international forest certification organisation.
All our titles that are printed on Greenpeace approved FSC certified paper
carry the FSC logo. Our paper procurement policy can be found at
www.rbooks.co.uk/environment

Mixed Sources
Product group from well-managed
forests and other controlled sources
www.fsc.org Cert no. TT-COC-2139
© 1996 Forest Stewardship Council
FSC

Designed and set by seagulls.net

Printed in the UK by CPI Mackays, Chatham, ME5 8TD

ISBN 9780091937577

To buy books by your favourite authors and register for offers visit
www.rbooks.co.uk

For E.B. Wallace
Whom we love very, very much

INTRODUCTION

ello. My name's Danny Wallace, and I am a man. Not just that – I've been a man all my life, and I intend to keep it up, too.

This book is, I hope, a modest attempt at capturing the incredible wonder and glorious majesty of being a man in the twenty-first century. Most of the stories are specific to me. But hopefully that means they'll somehow be specific to you as well. Whether you're a man yourself, or even if you just met one, once.

So what follows pretty much represents the story of my life over the past year-and-a-bit. A year in which I had a pint with a man I did not know. A year in which I was discovered by my wife to be a secret pyjama wearer. A year in which I was forced to eject a minor celebrity from a party, found myself naked in a shower with a stranger, turned up to places too late, turned up to places too early, was mistaken for the black film actor Danny Glover, realised I didn't know how to walk behind women at night, discovered the finest sandwich known to man, was taken for a deaf man in a chip shop, found that staring at children is frowned upon, and had a heated disagreement with a bishop.

But in among the trials and trips and stumbles and fumbles are moments of glorious *triumph*, too. Moments where the blushes are vanquished or the pride reinstated. *Those* are the moments that make our Awkward Situations for Men – mine and yours and everyone else's – something close to worthwhile.

A few thanks … First of all my undying gratitude to all those at *ShortList* magazine – particularly Phil Hilton – for allowing me to incorporate many of the columns I've written for them. To Lisa Thomas, for making that column happen in the first place. And, of course, my huge and sincere thanks to my wife, my friends, and the two or three pals who *are* my friend Colin …

See you in there.

Danny

AND SO WE BEGIN...

I am at the age where my friends are suddenly having children. I have even been asked to be a godfather, although I am still learning the rules of what you can and can't say.

Recently, one friend was telling me about his baby boy.

'He's got a new sound that he does,' he said, looking tired and pale. 'He just sits there and goes NYUP. NYUP. NYUP. For hours and hours. He was making it *all* last night. NYUP. NYUP. NYUP.'

He smiled, weakly, in a 'What can you do?' kind of way. I tried to sympathise.

'He sounds like a *dick*,' I said.

My friend just looked at me.

'But he *did*,' I said to my wife, as she silently collected our things.

SPRING

THE SANDWICH

I am standing on the high street as the drizzle soaks through my jacket on a fine British spring afternoon, and I am staring – bewildered and alone – into the middle distance.

I have just taken a bite of the finest sandwich I have ever tasted; perhaps, even, the finest sandwich ever made.

'There was lettuce involved,' I tell my friend Colin, later, my wild eyes shining as I relive it. 'And some kind of … *sauce*.'

Colin looks amazed. Later, I am sure, his amazement will turn to jealousy. But for now, we are just two men talking about an incredible sandwich.

I had been in the queue at Subway when it happened. Usually, like millions of other dull and unimaginative men, I would order a Sweet Onion Chicken Teriyaki sub. It is what I normally do. It is predictable. Safe. *Trusted*. I know where I am with a Sweet Onion Chicken Teriyaki sub, and it is usually just outside Subway with sauce down my top and a piece of tomato on my shoe.

But not today, my friends. Oh, no. Today was *different*.

I'd been in a hurry. I had a train to catch. Things to do. And the queue was moving slowly.

In front of me, a man in a black leather jacket was taking his time. Not for him the simplicity and ease of choosing a pre-designed sandwich. No. He was going *off-menu*. Improvising a new and elaborate creation. He was a lunchtime maverick, operating outside the boundaries, like a law unto himself. I watched as he selected his ingredients, mixed and matched, chose the perfect bread and then the right sauce. He added a little cheese, I think, and certainly a smattering of jalapenos. He asked for some salt and pepper, and requested it not be toasted, and then he made the server take out some of the lettuce, because it was 'just too much'.

At first, I was annoyed at the man.

Who *is* this clown? I thought. Who does he think he is, laughing in the face of sandwich convention? Why does he not simply order a Sweet Onion Chicken Teriyaki sandwich like the rest of us?

But I maintained my dignified silence. Soon he would be finished, and I would finally be able to order my drab and soulless lunch.

'Ah, hang on,' I suddenly hear him say. 'That's not what I asked for – I asked for the six-incher. Not the whole sub. I told you that.'

There is a slight harrumph from the server, who mutters something about not being told to stop, and a sigh is passed down the queue as we realise our wait will be extended by a few more seconds. I look at my watch. And I think of my train. And I suddenly say, 'Look, *I'll* have the other half. I don't mind. I just want to get out of here.'

The man smiles at me, and says, 'Are you sure?', and I nod graciously but with eyes closed to indicate that this is an *extraordinary* gesture on my part. He leaves with his six-incher, and I watch him head into M&S, and then I pay for mine and hurry along the street towards the tube.

And it is there, on the high street, that I take my first bite.

'It was a taste *sensation*,' I tell Colin. 'Light without being frivolous. Substantial without being overbearing. It was a thing of such beauty that words cannot do it justice.'

'Who was he?' asks Colin. 'Who *was* this man?'

'Who knows?' I say. 'But oh, what taste he has! He probably drives a classic Jag, and drinks freshly brewed coffee on his Eames chair while his supermodel girlfriend naps on the Chesterfield! He probably has a cat named something classical, and a favourite red wine! I bet he uses moisturiser and summers in Italy!'

'Definitely!' said Colin, wide-eyed. 'If his Subway sandwich is anything to go by!'

In that moment, I wanted to *be* that man. A plan started to form in my head. I would hang around in Subway all day from now on, and when he eventually walked in and ordered his sandwich, I would start to constantly follow him round. I would follow him into out-of-the-way but achingly cool little cafes that I would never have found, or designer boutiques that I never knew existed, and I would buy *exactly* what *he* did. I would trail him from aisle to aisle in the supermarket, picking up pasta sauces I'd never tried because I'd always bought Dolmio, or cocoa beans from the Andes which I'd never tried because I'd always just bought a Twix. I would be this man's copycat, and he my guru. It would work. It *had* to. Because that sandwich was bloody *incredible*.

'Imagine the museums I'll go to!' I said to Colin. 'Imagine the *people* I'll meet! The things I'll *see*!'

'And you're sure this bloke won't mind you following him around all the time?'

'He'll never know! And if he does, I'm sure that we will become great friends. He will see in me a soulmate to mentor. We will be united by exquisite taste.'

'We should go to Subway,' said Colin, suddenly. 'Maybe you can re-create that sandwich!'

I laugh, and shake my head. Poor, simple Colin. If only life were that easy, I think. Alas, it is not.

For a few days, I think about the man in Subway and his incredible sandwich. And then, one day, a week or so later, I spot him again, striding down the street with a Starbucks panini in his hand.

And my heart stops.

He is wearing the worst trousers I have ever seen. Bright red slacks with stupid pockets. The sort of trousers you'd buy in M&S on a dull and grey Wednesday afternoon after you've just been all picky in Subway. I am shattered.

Later that week, I return to Subway.

I wait quietly, and then say, 'Chicken Teriyaki, please.'

THE DIVERSION

t is a glorious day, and I am sitting in a cab in mild traffic, somewhere in central London, when I look out of the window and see someone I know.

It's his day off, and he is enjoying a coffee in the mid-morning sun, alone and relaxing with the paper, and he seems to be very content indeed.

The cab creeps forward, but only a few feet, and I decide to give him a ring to let him know I'm staring straight at him. He will be surprised and delighted, and we will do that thing that people do when they're on the phone and can see each other, where we make big exaggerated faces and wave a lot.

I get my phone out as the cab inches forward again. I look up. The lights are on red, but I cannot miss my opportunity. This has to happen *now*.

I scroll through until I find his name, and then I press 'call'. I stifle a giggle. I try and catch the cabbie's eye in the rear-view mirror. He will not *believe* this. What a coincidence! Two people who know each other, quite near each other! But the cabbie is listening to Jon Gaunt on talkSPORT shouting about immigrants and thus probably not in the market for friend-based whimsy.

The call connects and I hear the ringtone. I watch, a smile plastered right across my face, as immediately, my friend lowers his newspaper, takes a sip of his coffee, and reaches into his pocket for his phone.

I try and come up with a witty thing to say when he picks up.

Maybe I'll start with a wry, 'Enjoying your coffee?' and then he will laugh, and then look startled, because how did I know? Or maybe I'll say, 'Hey, what's in the *newspaper*?' and that would be funny too, because *how did I know* he had a newspaper?

I chuckle and decide to just go with the moment and follow my heart, and there is a tense moment as the ring-ring continues, and my friend has to turn his phone the right way round, and now he's looking at the screen, and he can see my name, and he's not smiling yet but he *will* be, and he finds the right button, and he ...

Oh.

'Hello, I'm unable to take your call right now. Please do leave a message after the beep.'

Eh?

There's been some kind of mistake! It's gone straight to answerphone! He must've accidentally pressed 'Divert'!

I stare at my friend, and I blink a couple of times. He puts his phone away and shakes his paper, and picks up his coffee and takes a long sip.

And like that, I am dismissed.

Beep.

I am startled. What do I say? What message do I leave? I can't say, 'Are you enjoying your coffee?' Who knows *when* he'll listen to this? What if he's nowhere *near* a coffee? I'll sound *mental*. Do I tell him I could see him? But then he'll know he rebuffed me! And he'll know *I know* he rebuffed me!

'Hi!' I say, and then I clear my throat. 'Yes ... me here. Danny. Just phoning to ... you know ... say ... I hope ... newspaper's good.'

I hang up. *Newspaper's good?* What the hell does *that* mean?

And then the lights change, and the cab roars into action, and we move off through the streets of Soho, leaving my friend and his coffee far behind.

'It's hard to argue with him, isn't it?' says the cabbie, but he's referring to Jon Gaunt, who is *very* easy to argue with, because he's always wrong.

'Yes,' I say, but I am still thinking about my friend. How *dare* he decline my call? It was a *nice* call! It was a call of friendship and coincidence! And it's not like he was busy! He was sitting outside drinking a latte and reading the *Mirror*, grateful for a few moments to himself on his one day off of the week! That's *exactly* the right time for a pointless call!

I suddenly realise something with horror. All those calls I've ever made to all those people that haven't been picked up … all those times the phone has rung out, or gone to answerphone, or not rung *quite enough times* to convincingly have gone to answer-phone … what if I was *rebuffed each time*? What if they *weren't* just busy, or they *hadn't* just left their mobile in another room, or it *wasn't* that they were simply running out of battery? What if each one was a conscious *decision*? A decision weighed up in mere *seconds*? What if I was a *constant rebuffee*?

There was no way of knowing. I had to assume the worst. I was an outcast. I'd witnessed it. I was a man from whom it was not worth taking a phone call.

I am filled with embarrassment and annoyance at my mate. I want to call him and have it out, but what if he doesn't answer? He'd win *again*! I frown. You can't treat friends like that. In fact, I pompously decide, you can't treat *human beings* like that. It should be against the law. I vow to write to some kind of European MP about this, but then I hear Jon Gaunt saying that you can't trust European MPs as far as you can throw them, and I am filled with hatred and annoyance for the world, and I agree with Jon Gaunt, because when you feel like that it's hard not to.

My phone rings.

Ha! I think. It is *him*. He's finished his coffee and, flushed with guilt and regret, he wishes to apologise for not picking up. I fish the phone out of my pocket and look at it. How should I react to one so heinous?

But it is not him. It is my friend Colin.

I press 'Divert', and I silently fume, all the way home.

FISHING

There are three of us in a rented Vauxhall Astra, pulling into the driveway of the Perthshire cottage in which we'll be spending the next two days. Our assorted womenfolk will be joining us later … and it is our intention to impress them.

'We'll *catch* our dinner!' says Richard, and Marc and I look at him in awe.

'What, like a deer or something?' I say.

'No!' says Richard. 'We will *fish*! We will immerse ourselves in that most noble of battles – the battle betwixt man and fish – and we will *win*!'

'Yes!' says Marc.

'Stupid fish!' I say. 'They will rue the day!'

Richard goes off to find a fishing rod, and I sit down with the book Marc has given me as a holiday present. It is entitled *The Book of Predictions*, by Irving Wallace, Amy Wallace, and a bloke whose name *used* to be Wallace but who inexplicably changed it to Wallechinsky. Those are the *worst* type of Wallace. Sometimes I think we should take them off the mailing list. The book was written in 1981 and features a variety of different experts predicting how the future will turn out. It is possibly the most fascinating book I have ever read.

'By 1988', it screams, the US will have destroyed the Soviet Union 'along with 100,000,000 Soviet citizens', prompting the UN to set up new headquarters on the moon. The world will be brought to its knees in the early 1990s because of the terrifying war between Iceland and Malta. Basketball will be stopped because we are all so tall that people grow weary of watching burly giants stuffing small balls into tiny nets. A computer will make its own scientific discovery in 1989 and be nominated for the Nobel Prize! Robots will clash in space! All disease solved by '91!

How exciting the future used to be!

'Are you going to sit there reading all day, or are you going to be a man?' asks Marc, suddenly there. I put the book down. I am going to be a man!

We stand, the three of us, facing our old enemy – the sea. None of us has really fished before, but how hard can it be? Not as hard as it will be when all fish die, in 1993, that's for sure.

We cast our newly untangled line into the water. It goes maybe four feet. This is fine for now. Subtlety is key: get the fish used to the idea of a line, and then strike like the panther. But nothing happens for a very long time and we get bored. Suddenly, Marc remembers something.

'We're supposed to use bait, aren't we?' he says.

'Bring me a worm!' yells Richard. 'And I will bring you a fish!'

We all feel really manly – just as this weekend was intended to make us feel. Marc runs off to fetch a spade and I pick up my book again. The strange thing about the future, I think, wisely, is that it's always thrilling until you're old enough to realise that none of it has happened yet. It's almost as if no one's *bothering* to work on the technology to bring us magic carpets any more.

'This is the best I could do,' says Marc, holding the United Kingdom's smallest worm. Richard attaches it to the hook and flicks the line back into the water. The line goes four feet again. The worm goes considerably further.

'What else can we use as bait?' says Richard. The only food we've brought to the cottage is what we bought at a delicatessen seventy miles away. It is not traditional fish bait.

'Do fish like cheese?' I ask. 'Or prosciutto? We've got a lot of prosciutto.'

'Olives?' asks Marc, and we all laugh at him, because that's stupid.

'Bring me some speck!' shouts Richard, who really is becoming a man.

Marc and I run off and fetch some speck and a Portobello mushroom. We are suddenly in a rubbish, middle-class version of *City Slickers*, but we are doing our best, and that is the mark of a man.

'Will speck work?' I ask, panicking that we will lose our battle with the fish, of which we've seen nothing.

Richard looks at me, calmly.

'Danny, speck is cold-smoked slowly and intermittently for two or three hours a day for a period of roughly a week using woods such as beech at temperatures that never exceed twenty degrees Celsius,' he says. 'If they don't eat it, they're idiots.'

Marc says nothing, but closes his eyes and nods slowly.

Two hours later, we've used up most of our speck, and Marc has dropped and trodden on the Portobello mushroom. We've seen and caught nothing. The girls arrive in their jeep.

'What's for dinner?' they say.

I attempt to distract them.

'Did you know that by 1985, shortages and high prices of dairy products will lead to intense new interest in soybeans?'

I am ignored.

'Are you fishing ... with *olives*?' asks my wife.

'No,' we say.

We put our fishing rod and olives down and sheepishly join the girls, who have brought meat, and vegetables, and breads. I realise we are not men. We are boys. And no matter what we were told when we were kids, we will never be men. We will just be large, ungainly children. This has always been the future.

'Oh, look!' says Richard's wife, as we reach the cottage.

A fish has just made a beautiful, arcing leap, splashing down on to the otherwise calm, sun-dappled, early-evening waters.

Richard, Marc and I look at each other, vexed. I put my book away.

I could have predicted that would happen.

THE ANECDOTE

And then he sort of stumbled backwards,' I say, to the small crowd around me, who are listening, rapt, to my every word. 'And he *fell into the bath*!'

I finish my short performance by pointing at an imaginary bathtub and raising my eyebrows in mock disbelief. There is nice, good-natured laughter from my tiny audience, who have been listening to this story, and waiting for this punchline, for the last several minutes. I relax, knowing I have done my bit. I have made my contribution to the party and now I can stand back and let someone else tell a story, safe in the knowledge that I will, for the rest of the evening, be known as the bloke who said that thing about his mate who fell into the bath.

But then one of them says, 'And *then* what happened?'

I am startled. I had not been expecting that. Traditionally, that story has always ended with me saying, 'And he fell into the bath!' and then pointing at an imaginary bathtub and raising my eyebrows, but now all eyes are on me. I am momentarily thrown and as I glance around at the expectant faces before me I don't know what to say.

'Basically,' says Colin, suddenly back from the buffet and witnessing my humiliation, 'his wife was absolutely *furious* with him ...'

The crowd begins to chuckle again. I turn to see Colin's face light up.

'Particularly as Steve was still wearing his *pyjamas* at the time ...'

The reaction is huge. The story has gone better than it has ever gone before. The idea of a furious wife and some wet pyjamas is almost too much for them to bear. One lady is doing one of those silent laughs where all they do is shake a lot with their eyes closed, and another gentleman just points at Colin and shouts 'HA!' before adding a little thumbs-up and walking off, waving his hands in glorious disbelief. Soon we are on our own and I turn to confront Colin.

'What did you do *that* for?' I say, shrugging in as angry a way as I can muster.

'Do what? I was helping you out!' he says. 'You were clearly struggling!'

'But you *know* Steve's wife wasn't there when he fell into the bath! And he *wasn't* in his pyjamas! What did you say he was in his pyjamas for?'

'It was just a little flourish,' he says. 'Just a little something to help the story along!'

'But the story didn't *need* helping along! It was fine as it was! He stumbled and fell into the bath! It's funny!'

'It's not *that* funny,' says Colin, with pity in his eyes. 'It's just a man falling into a bath.'

'Sometimes less is more,' I say, defensively, but we are distracted by a man with ginger hair who's sidling past. He raises a carrot baton to Colin as a mark of deep respect, and mouths 'Pyjamas' with a grin. Colin smiles, smugly, and nods and rolls *his* eyes too. The man starts laughing again and moves on.

I consider what I'm seeing. The pyjamas element certainly does seem to have taken the story to a new level. Perhaps pyjama stories are the zeitgeist. But I am now very concerned indeed that *none* of my stories is good enough. That I will need to bring Colin with me everywhere I go to improvise new endings to established favourites. Suddenly I lack any confidence whatsoever in my party ammunition. The landscape has changed. I am bereft of bankers.

'You can't *do* that,' I say, testily. 'You can't just go about improving other people's stories. It's irresponsible.'

'Why is that irresponsible?'

'Because now all those people will be wondering why I didn't mention the fact that Steve was wearing pyjamas in the first place. They will think I am an inept storyteller incapable of including the most basic of facts.'

'I suppose you *should* have mentioned it. It *was* the funniest bit.'

'But he *wasn't* wearing pyjamas! And now I have to remember that he *was* wearing pyjamas *and* that his wife was furious. *That's* why it's irresponsible!'

'I thought I was helping!' says Colin, looking genuinely hurt. 'To be honest, I've never liked that story anyway. I've always thought it was ... laboured.'

I am shocked. *Laboured*? Colin has always thought the Steve-falling-into-the-bath story was *laboured*? It is a classic of its time! Well, this has certainly been a day for testing all my preconceptions! Perhaps the world *is* flat after all! *Anything* is possible if the Steve-falling-into-the-bath story is *laboured*!

I shake my head at Colin and resolve to prove him wrong. I spot a man I've not yet talked to, standing by the window on his own, eating a samosa. I show Colin my stern face and I nod at him to let him know I have accepted his unspoken challenge. Laboured, indeed! I wander over to the man and within minutes I have managed to steer the conversation round to baths and bathing.

'Actually, I've got a funny story about that,' I say, a little too loudly, glancing over at Colin.

The story does not go well.

Colin walks by, just in time to hear the words 'wife', 'pyjamas' and 'pineapple'.

'Was the pineapple too much?' I ask, later, and Colin nods.

'Sometimes less is more,' he says.

THE BABY

Remember to be on your best behaviour,' says my wife, a little unnecessarily.

After what happened in the same place recently, I do not need reminding to be on my best behaviour. All I can *think* about is how I should be on my best behaviour.

We park the car outside our friend's house and can already see them through the window. They're everywhere.

Kids. Toddlers. Babies. Scampering about. Pushing each other over. Wiping food into the carpets. Blaming each other for minor misdemeanours and then bursting into tears.

'Remember!' says my wife, her finger in the air.

'I'll be fine!' I say, closing my eyes and nodding in the way I've seen people do on TV when they're trying to be comforting.

And then we ring the doorbell.

While we're waiting for someone to answer, I may as well tell you the little thing that happened, a couple of years before, at a party at the same house – though you should stop me if you've heard it.

We'd been in the garden, and I'd looked down to see a small boy kicking my shins. He was persistent and showed a keen talent for it, but after a while enough was enough. I found a piece of paper and wrote out a note I asked him to give to his father, who was getting gently sozzled nearby. The little boy had obliged and handed his dad the note. It was then that I realised this was probably a bad idea. His dad, now no longer merely *gently* sozzled, appeared to forget his son did not yet possess the ability to write, and genuinely seemed to believe he'd managed to scrawl 'I am pissed off my tiny tits' himself. Now the angry father wanted to know who'd apparently been feeding his child alcohol. He soon decided it was me. I learned that night what it is to cause a scene, and have never again implied a child is high on booze.

'Hello!' says our friend, answering the door. 'Come in!'

We do as she says and are soon sitting at her table, the smell of good food around us, laughter everywhere. But no kids, all of a sudden.

'Where are all the children?' asks one of our fellow guests, concerned for her four-year-old.

'I think they're in the upstairs loo,' I say, smiling, and then I freeze.

Stop.

Stop.

I take a deep breath. I'd been *about* to say, 'I think they're in the upstairs loo, having a fag out the window.'

But why? *Why* had I thought that would be a good thing to say? It was *not* a good thing to say! Still, I'd managed to stop myself – that was me remembering to be on my best behaviour!

And then my wife kicks me under the table, gently, because as it turns out, 'I think they're in the upstairs loo' is *still* a very odd thing to say when you don't then explain why you've said it.

I take a sip of my wine as the lady fakes an uncomfortable ha-ha, pretends to relax, and then gets up and jogs for the stairs. My wife shoots me a look, and I lean over.

'I'd been *about* to say "having a fag out the window",' and I wink at her, and she looks at me understandingly, and pats my hand to show me how proud she is of me *not* saying that. I smile to myself. I have done well. I will not be asked to leave *this* time round. I will be causing no scenes.

And then a lady sits down next to us carrying her lovely, blond-haired, blue-eyed baby. He smiles at me, and I make the silly face I make at little children, and he giggles. I am doing *so* well today, I think.

The lady – an actress – talks to us as she feeds him blueberries. I stop listening to the conversation as I watch him ravenously push blueberry after blueberry into his little face. He polishes them all off, and then starts to swing his right arm about, because he wants more, but his mum's not listening, because she's talking to my wife about car alarms, and the baby keeps on swinging his arm, and then I notice he's got a tiny, square piece of blueberry skin stuck to his top lip, just under his nose, and as he swings and swings and looks grumpier and grumpier, the little black square stays put, and then I laugh very loudly, and everyone stops what they're doing, and I forget myself and I say, 'Your baby looks *just* like Hitler!'

I smile broadly.

My wife closes her eyes.

I stop smiling.

THE RULES

t struck me, just a few days ago, how many rules I have inadvertently applied to my life. Rules I did not know I had. Rules I did not know I needed.

It happened as I was walking past McDonald's, and there it was: a bright and giant poster of a perfectly formed Big Mac, its light American cheese in the first few glorious seconds of melting, its lettuce crisp and bright and green, its tomatoes dappled by health-inducing dew.

Big Macs are *amazing*, I thought to myself. Look at that!

I stared at its huge, confident goodness. At its three-part sesame-seeded bun. At the sexy hint of special Big Mac sauce, revealing only a moment of itself, flirting with me, willing me in. And then, as my tastebuds began to stir, and my tummy rumbled in anticipation, I tore myself away, and I strode on down the street.

No, I thought. No Big Macs for you. It's a Tuesday. And you had those Chicken McNuggets on Friday. At least *one week* must pass between individual McDonald's. You *know* that.

At the corner, moments later, and holding a dry and wilting hummus and pepper sandwich with organic fennel wheat-free bread, I passed my local.

Imagine if I'd had a Big Mac, I thought. Imagine if I'd had a Big Mac instead of this dry and wilting hummus and pepper sandwich with organic fennel wheat-free bread. I could have a *pint* now. How *nice* a pint would be after a Big Mac!

I looked at my watch.

But no, I thought. No pints for you. It is 11.57 in the morning, and as such not an appropriate time for a pint. For that would be *morning* drinking, and morning drinking must be *frowned* upon.

At home, I took a sip of my spinach, parsley, celery and carrot smoothie-juice with Echinacea and wheatgrass boosters, and noticed that *Loose Women* was on.

I could just watch a *bit*, I thought. Just to find out what their take is on the important issues of the day. And then maybe see who the guest is. Perhaps Jackie Brambles will be interviewing Danny John-Jules about a bad play he's in.

And then I snapped out of it.

No, I thought. No *Loose Women* for you. For it is the middle of the day, and there is *work* to be done. The middle of the day is no place for *Loose Women*.

And then I watched for half an hour anyway.

Why must these rules blight my life? I thought, wandering downstairs, laden down with guilt, the thoughts and philosophies of Carol McGiffin still ringing in my ears. Why must there *be* such rules? Why can I not spend my days eating Big Macs and watching inappropriate television? Is it merely because I am neither a student nor pregnant? Surely that is *discrimination*!

I got on with my work.

But the next day, something had changed.

I am taking the day off! I thought, as I lay in bed. Today will be a day of freedom! Of fun! Of breaking the rules! Just like I used to! Before there were any rules to break! Today will be the day … I eat a Big Mac!

I immediately call Colin.

'Colin! It's me! Let's have a Big Mac!'

'What? Eh? Why?'

'Because it is time to break the rules!'

'*What* rules?'

'You know! *The rules*! You *must* have some!'

'There are no rules to McDonald's, my friend,' says Colin. 'Just as there are no rules to love or war.'

'What about the once-a-week rule?'

'Oh yeah, there's *that* rule.'

'Come on! Let's set out on a brave, day-long adventure! We could do something *crazy*! We could go to *Pizza Hut*! Or we could order a bottle of wine somewhere and when they say, "Do you want some water for the table?" we could say "No!".'

'I like it!' says Colin. 'We could purposely *not* eat our five-a-day!'

'Yes! Or eat more salt than is good for us! We could shovel salt into our mouths while watching *Come Dine with Me* in the *middle of the day*!'

I was excited now.

'So shall we do it?' I said. 'Shall we *not* drink two litres of water today? Shall we purposely skip breakfast? Shall we avoid walking briskly? Shall we *do* it, Colin?'

'We shall!' he says. 'Who wants to eat *bran*? It's *madness*! So when? When do we do it?'

'Today!' I shout, pointing my finger in the air. 'Carpe diem, Colin! *Carpe diem*! Big Mac *City*!'

'I AM *LOVIN'* IT!' he yells, cleverly. 'But today is *Wednesday*. I go to the *gym* on Wednesdays. And also, tonight is *The Apprentice*, and I always watch that with Jo. It's like a *rule*.'

'Right.'

'Another day, though.'

'Yes. Another day.'

But no. Today is the day. Because *I* am a bloody *maverick*, and my rules are there for the *breaking* ...

I have passion in my eyes and a fire in my belly. I am Danny Wallace – social maverick. It has been decided: today, *I will eat a Big Mac*!

I leave the house, thrilled by my own bravery. I am a man! I am a man reclaiming my manhood! Not for me the petty guidelines, protocols and etiquette of modern-day living! Not for me the constant worries about whether my behaviour is frowned upon! Why *should* my bananas be Fairtrade? Who *needs* a dramatic focal point in their living room? Who *cares* if my carrot batons are organic?

I check my watch. It is 10.19am. I know what to do. I head for the pub.

You see? I think, smiling as I carry my illicit pint outside. I am not alone in this!

My eyes scan the tables around me. There are men here. Real men. Men who do not worry about how others see them. Each has a pint and is staring into the middle distance, lost, probably, in thoughts similar to mine. On any other day, of course, they may just look like loners, hunched over sad morning pints on the fringes of society. But not to me. To me they look like *comrades*. OK, so one of them is talking to his feet. But none of them looks like they're concerned about how much bran they're eating, or whether or not a can of Tango counts as part of their five-a-day. And today, nor do I. I sip at my lager. It tastes strange so early in the morning. But perhaps this is merely the taste of freedom. A taste I have not tasted in quite some time.

I sit, quietly, revelling in my liberty. But like the Littlest Hobo, I must keep moving on. I try to catch the eye of the man nearest me as I leave. To perhaps raise a single eyebrow at him and exchange a glance of precious solidarity. But he is still talking to his feet, and so I leave it. But he knows.

On I walk – slowly, not briskly – to the high street. I pass McDonald's. *Not yet*, I think. *Not yet, my little friend.*

What could I do? I think. I'm supposed to be at home, working! Being healthy! Being responsible! But I could do anything! Go anywhere! I could walk into a travel agents and buy a ticket somewhere – and then not go! Or I could hail a taxi and say 'Follow that cab!' and then follow one, with little regard to purpose or money! Who knows where I could end up? Limehouse? Wealdstone? Dalston? The world is my rule-free oyster!

In the end, I buy a Twix and go to Currys.

I shouldn't be in here, I think, naughtily. There is nothing I need! Those TV programmes are always telling you you shouldn't go into places like this when you don't have a purpose! You'll end up buying something you'll regret!

I browse for a bit, but Currys is actually quite boring. I will not allow that to beat me, though. I buy a hundred Verbatim CD-R discs for £11.99 – even though I *know* I can get the same ones cheaper at the market! Ha. Poor Colin, missing a day like this, I think. A day of impulse and rule-breakery. He will not believe his ears when I tell him what I've done.

I pass the cinema. I never go into the cinema on my own. It is not the done thing. People who go to the cinema on their own during the day are seen as oddballs. It is against the rules. I know there and then that I will go.

But first ...

'Big Mac, please.'

'Big Mac meal?'

'Yes, please.'

'Drink?'

'Coke, please.'

'Coke or Diet Coke?'

'Coke!'

I sneak the Big Mac meal into the cinema inside my bag. The ushers know this but do not seem to care. *This is insanity!* I think to myself, shaking my head and nestling into my seat. The film begins, and it is rubbish. I have no one to make sarcastic comments to. There are two or three other lone men watching the film. I eat my Big Mac in bored silence, and instantly feel a little ill. Also, the pint has made me sleepy and I'm fairly sure my Twix was off.

I leave the cinema disappointed. I look around me and try to come up with another rule to break. Another rule that so-called society and guilt tell me is set in stone. I am looking for quite some time.

I am home by three o'clock, my initial feelings of rebellion dampened. I smell of Big Mac. I've Sky+'d *Loose Women*, and I try to watch it, but Kerry Katona is on and so I switch it off.

I have a nap.

When I wake, I eat an organic carrot baton and decide I quite like having rules. And then I sit on the sofa and wait for my wife to come home, so we can watch *The Apprentice* together.

STAGEFRIGHT

My friend Graham once told me that if you're ever standing at a urinal and you find yourself suddenly unable to let go, you should not panic. Panicking is the very worst thing you can do at that point. Apart from looking at the man next to you and saying 'I can't pee!'.

No, he said, what you need to do is use everything within you to picture in your mind's eye yourself in full flow ... before you imagine turning and peeing on the trousers and shoes of the man next to you.

And it *works*. It works very *well*.

But right now, it *wasn't* working.

I didn't know what it was. I'd been imagining peeing on the shoes of the man next to me for what seemed like *hours*.

I'd entered the toilets full of hope, and optimism, and, more importantly, beer. This was standard procedure. I'd peed literally *dozens* of times before. I knew how to do it, and I considered myself bloody good at it. OK, I'm no professional, but you'd be hard pressed to find a keener amateur. I practise every day.

But there was just something about the timing of this situation that had been off. I'd arrived just as the man next to me – the only other man present – was doing really well, polishing off an expert pee that was now reaching its final, dramatic act and building towards a powerful conclusion. Somehow, starting to pee now would be rude; like I was some young upstart attempting to upstage a master. But then he finished with a flourish and subconsciously handed me the baton. Which I assure you is *not* a euphemism.

I felt now was my time. Everything was in place – me, the urinal, *everything*. The man left and I was free to begin, alone and at peace.

But nothing was happening. Never mind. Just relax. Relax. Relax and let nature take its course. I let my eyes wander towards the ceiling. By which I mean I looked up, not that I have magic, walking eyes.

But still nothing. What was going *on*?

And then: a controversial event.

Someone walked in. I didn't turn round. I just concentrated on what I had to do. But I was unnerved. Any progress I'd been making had been instantly beaten back.

A man took his place at the urinal next to me and undid his zipper. He cleared his throat and stared straight ahead. I did the same. But all this did was draw attention to the fact that I was not peeing. Oh God. I was *still* not peeing. We were standing in total silence, and I was *not peeing*. The man had no idea how long I'd been in here. I could've been in here not peeing for *days*! Instantly, I knew one thing. I had to *beat* this man at peeing. I had to pee *first*. If *he* peed first, there'd be no *way* I could start peeing. And then I'd have to not pee while waiting for him to stop peeing! And then he'd walk off, knowing that I'd been standing there, not peeing! He'd tell all his mates that I was rubbish at peeing, and they'd all look at me and snigger as I walked back in, and I'd have to do something clever, like shout 'I just peed!' when I got back inside.

But nothing was happening. *Nothing*.

And I knew – I just *knew* – that any second now, with grim inevitability, the man next to me was about to get things going, about to release a fast-flowing river of such crystal beauty that I would weep when I saw it. I wanted to give up, and pretend I'd done what I'd been there to do, and do my zipper up, and wash my hands, but it's impossible to fake this convincingly.

And then I realised. It was still silent. *He* couldn't go *either*.

Now *this* was *worse*. Now we were locked in an embarrassing battle that neither of us wanted any part of. *He* couldn't pee, and *I* couldn't pee, and *he knew I knew* we couldn't pee. The only thing that would save this was if *one* of us could pee. *Anything* would do. The tiniest trickle. A momentary release. Anything that either one of us could justify as a pee would save us *both* from this urinal torture.

I remembered Graham, and imagined myself turning round and peeing freely on this man's shoes. But I'm a polite man, and I then had to imagine apologising to him, and offering to buy him new shoes.

We continued to stand in painful, pained silence. He cleared his throat again. Oh my God, we could be here for the rest of our *lives*. Someone had to *do* something!

And then: the bang of the door against the wall once more. A loud and confident entrance. Whoever this was, he'd have *no* trouble peeing. He'd probably been peeing all the way up the stairs. He'd probably won *awards*.

Now there was a *new* fix. There were only two urinals. The new challenger was now leaning back against the wall, waiting for us to finish. But all he could hear was the sound of silence. No one was peeing. Nothing was happening. What were The Rules here? Surely new etiquette comes into play?

And that was when, with no warning or collusion whatsoever, me and the man next to me suddenly pretended to finish, did our zippers up, silently moved to the sink, washed our hands, dried them with towels, and walked out the door.

The new man watched us as we left. He *knew* there was something odd about what had happened, but he couldn't work out *what*.

My opponent and I were now *comrades*. We'd been through terror together. We had a *secret*. We both sat down with our separate parties and tried to ignore each other.

Ten minutes later, I got up to go to the toilet. As I did so, I noticed him in front of me, heading through the door.

I let him go first.

WALKING

ever tip-toe behind a strange woman on a dark street at night. This is what I'd been doing for the last twenty or thirty feet, and it really wasn't working out well at all. The problem is, I just don't know how to act when walking behind women at night. I *hate* it. I hate it so much I would rather ban all women than have to walk behind one after dark. That's right. *Ban* them.

This woman and I had turned on to the same side street at the same time.

It was a long road, and I was now technically following her.

I hate this, because I'm an idiot. I'm an idiot because I instantly assume this woman will feel intimidated by me. That she'll think I'm a crazy-eyed knife-wielding loon, or a stalker, or someone who wants to talk to her about God.

I tried to work out what I should do, and sped up, thinking perhaps I should overtake her, but then realised that would mean getting *closer*, and the last thing I wanted her to think was that I wanted to get *closer*.

So I slowed down again, and tried to come up with another plan.

The problem, I think, is that as men, we know we are constantly under suspicion. In an ideal and crimeless world, we'd all walk around arm in arm, smiling and tipping our hats. We'd skip gaily and step gingerly … but this was a street in North London approaching midnight, and as such, not somewhere I'd recommend skipping gaily or stepping gingerly. Even to gay skip-pers or ginger steppers.

If only I had a balloon, I thought, inexplicably, as I continued to follow this woman, self-conscious and bothered. If I had a balloon, she would look behind her and see a man with a balloon, and who's ever been attacked by a man with a balloon? Who'd 'attack' while holding a balloon? A balloon implies innocence, and fun. It would suggest I had just been somewhere *lovely*, perhaps the circus – or maybe I was *in* the circus! What woman would look behind her at night and be horrified to realise she was being followed by a huge clown?

Actually, that's *most* women, isn't it? Forget the balloon.

And then a thought struck me. I could make a noise! A noise which would signal that I *knew* I was following her, and that it didn't bother me in the least. A noise which would say, 'You and I, m'lady, are simply travellers along the same path. I mean you no harm.'

And so I coughed. And then cleared my throat. It was *genius*. By showing her I was there, I was alerting her to the fact that I had nothing to hide. But I wasn't sure she'd heard it, so I coughed again, louder. She appeared to speed up slightly. This wasn't good. Now she probably thought I was a crazy-eyed knife-wielding loon *with a cough*, and that was *worse*, because *nobody* wants a cough.

I decided the best course of action would be to slow down a bit and then keep as quiet as possible. And so I began to tread as carefully as I could, virtually tip-toeing down the street. I held my arms away from my sides, so that there'd be no chafing of sleeve against jacket. I made that weird nervous face you make when you're trying to be *really* quiet.

And then she slowed down and stopped under a streetlight on the corner of the road, and she started to look in her purse. This annoyed me for two reasons. One: I now had no option but to overtake her. I couldn't very well stop when *she* did. That would look *weird*. And two: why was she looking in her purse under a streetlight when she *knew* she was being followed by a coughing, knife-wielding loon? I felt like running up and bellowing at her just to teach her a lesson. What kind of society is it where women can walk down the street and fail to be intimidated by coughing, knife-wielding loons? It's political correctness gone mad.

And then I remembered that I was *not* a knife-wielding loon.

She was still rummaging through her bag as I got closer, but, not wishing to frighten her as I passed, I continued my slight tip-toe, complete with strange face.

And that was when she turned around. Turned around to see a man walking up very quietly behind her and making a strange face. We make eye contact. I see she is wearing earphones and has been oblivious to me the whole time.

I turn right at the junction and walk up another street, quietly cursing myself for extending my journey by ten minutes, and cursing society for making a man feel this way. Why had I overcompensated for my gender? Why had I assumed she would think I was an attacker? Wouldn't simply *not attacking her* have been good enough? Why can't everyone be as trusting as me? When will we understand that strangers are just friends you haven't met yet – even at night?

'Sorry, mate, have you got a light?' says a stranger round the corner. He is about my size, and he is a man.

'Nope!' I say, my voice suddenly higher than normal, and I scuttle away.

As I walk, I keep looking back, just in case he's tip-toeing behind me while making strange faces.

But he's miles away, and he just looks confused.

THE PROBLEM

Some men are not supposed to be good at talking about their problems. Others are supposed to be terrible listeners. I do my best to defy those rules.

Right now, in fact, I am sitting down with a friend who's just been through a rather harrowing break-up. His face is darkened by emotion. He hasn't touched his coffee. And now his tired and searching eyes are upon me, glistening with hope, seeking some of my ample wisdom. His words hang heavy in the air.

'So ... what do you think?'

I freeze slightly. As a good listener, I know all the moves. I've been nodding gently for the past ten or twenty minutes. Making concerned faces and shaking my head when it felt necessary or apt. But now I suddenly realise that all I've actually been doing while he's been detailing the precise and complex issues surrounding the breakdown of the most important and long-term relationship of his life is thinking: In the film *Ghostbusters*, Walter Peck was responsible for ordering the police to shut down the Ghostbusters' supernatural storage facility, resulting in the huge explosion which released hundreds of spirits on to the streets of Manhattan. But what agency did Walter Peck represent?

My friend's eyes are searching my blank and startled face. He thinks I'm mulling his problem over, but actually I'm wondering, Is there any way I can relate my advice to *Ghostbusters*?

'Because here's what *I* think ...' he says, and he's off again. That was close. But maybe he now suspects I wasn't listening. I lean in. *I'm going to listen this time*, I think. *I'm definitely going to listen.*

But as his voice lowers, I drift off again. The Environmental Protection Agency! I suddenly think. Of course! Walter Peck represented the *Environmental Protection Agency*! He was the busybody who inexplicably took against the Ghostbusters and their valuable work!

Brilliant. I've been trying to think of this for *ages*.

I subtly feel around my pocket for my phone, keeping a close eye on my friend. I have to time this right. I could just write 'EPA'. That would do it. That would mean that Colin knew I knew. But every time I lay my hands on my phone, my friend looks up at me, or raises his voice slightly in desperate anger at the injustice of his situation, and I have to pretend I was scratching.

Colin has been sending me questions about *Ghostbusters* all day. But not just *Ghostbusters* … *Ghostbusters 2*, as well. In my important position as one of Britain's least-known television personalities, sometimes I am asked to appear on TV shows in the name of charity. This time it's *Celebrity Mastermind*. When the researcher phoned up to ask me what my specialist chosen subject would be, I selected *Ghostbusters*. He told me that the other contestants were doing the French Revolution, the life and times of Tristram Shandy, and the history of Palestine. I thought about it, and then said I'd stick with *Ghostbusters*.

My phone vibrates again. Gah. That was probably Colin, mocking me because I didn't know that Walter Peck represented the EPA.

My friend looks up.

'You can get that if you like,' he says.

'No!' I say, loudly. 'It is important that we talk this out. That can wait.'

I feel quite proud of myself. Maybe I *am* a good listener. I wave my friend on, like a magnanimous king. He begins to talk. I look at my phone.

'Actually, I should just probably check it,' I say.

I stand up and move away. It's a text from Colin.

'What would happen if you crossed the streams?' it says.

I knew this. But what was the phrase? The *specific* phrase?

'First of all,' I write. 'Walter Peck was from the EPA.'

I smile to myself. It is good being cool.

I sit back down.

'Anyway, like I say, that's *my* take on it,' says my friend. 'But there's always option B ...'

'That's true,' I say, kindly. 'Option B.'

'So what's your conclusion?'

Um ...

'Well ... what's *your* conclusion?'

'I've just *told* you my conclusion. For, like, forty minutes.'

Right. This would take *skill*.

'Well, I think that you're right, and she's wrong,' I say. 'I think that relationships are like tricky onions. You can peel away the layers through analysing them, but if you peel too many away, eventually you're left with nothing. And also, relationships can make you cry, like onions can.'

My friend sits back, and gazes in wonder at my unique wisdom. I've done it! I'm a *great* listener – even when I'm not listening!

'Bravo,' he says, which is weird, because I didn't think *anyone* said 'bravo' any more.

'But back to the car,' he says. 'Option A or option B? Silver or black?'

'Oh. Er ... silver.'

'Because I think black.'

'That's what I think too.'

And then I consider how *lucky* it is that some men can't listen, and others can't talk.

'Hey,' I say. 'What happens if you cross the streams?'

'Total protonic reversal,' says my friend.

But it's also good that when it comes to the *really* important stuff, we're always there for each other.

SEX

am in the linen section of John Lewis with my wife when I realise we are lost.

'Don't panic,' I tell her, putting on my most reassuring face. 'We will survive this.'

It turns out my most reassuring face is also my most disconcerting.

I look around, trying to spot anyone who might be able to tell us how to get out of here, but our fellow shoppers seem as lost as we are, with their dead eyes and blank faces, listlessly picking up display cushions and holding them to the light, just for something to do.

And then I spot him. A shop attendant. A burly man with a haircut like Pob. He's got a clipboard and he's doing something important.

'Let's ask that man!' I say, loudly and quite gregariously, smiling as I do so to put him at his ease and encourage him to give us correct information. He looks around himself, in case I mean someone else, and so I point at him, and say, 'Excuse me, fella!'

I smile even more broadly this time, because I need this man's help. I've been putting on a brave face, but I cannot stress just how important it is that I am no longer in the linen section of John Lewis.

But as I bound over to him, he is frowning at me.

And then I realise.

He is a woman.

I am suddenly lost for words. What have I done? I think back to what I've just said.

Fella.

This is bad. This is very bad. This is worse than when I put my hand up at school and accidentally called my teacher 'Mum'.

But … maybe there's a way out. I mean, is 'fella' really a word that applies only to men?

Yes.

But surely, in these enlightened times, 'fella' can be just a friendly greeting. I mean, you can say 'guys', can't you, when you're referring to a mixed group? Maybe it's the same with 'fella'! Maybe I can get away with this! Maybe I can claim I was just being casual! 'Fella' doesn't have to mean 'male'! Who said anything about being *male*?

And then I remember that I *also* said, 'Let's ask that man.'

'We're just wondering how to get to the escalators …' says my wife, suddenly there, and all I can do is nod.

'Just over there,' says the lady, in a lady's voice, and she points one lady finger at a huge sign on which is quite clearly written 'escalators'. I notice she is wearing a lady's watch, which is smaller than a man's watch, because ladies have daintier eyes.

I should walk away now. I should thank her for her information and walk away. But I don't. Because I need to make it up to her. I need to make her believe that at no point did I doubt she was a lady.

Got it.

'Bright lights in here!' I say, pointing around me, and then I realise that's not really much of an explanation. In my head, it'd been brilliant. I'd been confused by the glare of the bright lights! I hadn't been thinking straight! I couldn't see properly! But I can tell she is having trouble reading between the lines of my complicated explanation. And besides, there are no bright lights in here, and if there *had've* been, I'd have obviously seen that she was a woman.

Maybe I should say, 'I mean it's quite dark.'

'Dan!' says my wife, lightly, standing by the escalators. 'Come on!'

She is like a patient owner summoning a stupid dog.

But I have not yet convinced this lady that I know she's a lady.

'I'm just saying about these lights in here,' I say, 'to this *lady*!'

Uh-oh. I think that sounded sarcastic.

'We'd better go, Dan …' says my wife, who I think might actually quite like to keep me on little reins, like a toddler.

'Thank you … madam,' I say, finally, and as seriously as I can, looking her straight in the eye.

'I *totally* got away with that,' I say to my wife, as we get to the top of the escalator.

'Definitely,' she says. 'There is no way a woman would notice someone in a shop shouting out that she was a man.'

I nod, but something about her tone makes me think she actually means the opposite. I have noticed people do this sometimes.

We walk into the shop next door. My wife stops a little too long to look at the toddler reins.

FRIENDS

t is nice, as a grown-up, to make new friends. I have just
made one. I'm sitting in a hotel bar in a foreign country,
late at night, with a man who just hours before was a mere
friend-of-a-friend. He is wearing a jaunty hat and a silk scarf,
which make him look like an eccentric rock star, and he is holding a glass of red wine and gesturing.

As you get older, it doesn't become *harder* to make new
friends. It just becomes a little less *necessary*. But when it happens,
when a connection is made almost despite yourself, it's no less
exciting than it was when you were nine.

'Check it out,' he suddenly says, pointing. 'A piano!'

'Yes!' I say. 'A piano!'

'Come on …' he says, getting up, and I follow him towards it.

This is brilliant, I am thinking. We're going to go and look at
a piano! Why do I never get up and look at pianos with any of my
normal friends? Perhaps we have lost the magic of friendship.
Maybe we have grown complacent, and it has taken a new friend
to make me realise this.

David sits down at the piano and starts to play a little tune.
It's good.

'*I* didn't know you could *play the piano*!' I say, in a way that
suggests I am utterly shocked that there could be something
in his biography that was unknown to me. And then I realise I
shouldn't be *that* shocked, given that just a few hours before
I didn't even know for sure if he had a face.

'Oh, yeah!' he says, and he begins to play harder, and more elaborately. A girl looks over and smiles.

'There's a girl looking at you and smiling!' I say, and David laughs.

'The food of love!' he says. He is very wise. It was about time I had a wise friend, I decide. I *deserve* one.

I smile and shake my head, and wander to a nearby sofa and sit down to patiently listen. Anything seems possible now. We are two new friends embarking on a wonderful journey of surprises together. David continues to play until the song is finished, and then he pauses for a moment, before starting another one entirely.

Oh! I think. He's doing another one.

It takes a moment or two for me to realise that this one is a love song. It is gentle, and romantic, and a couple at the far end of the bar look deep into each other's eyes.

That's nice, I think. David is being gregarious and talented, and it is uniting people.

And then David looks over at me and smiles. I smile back and raise my wine glass in his direction, as if to say, 'Well done, my new friend, on being gregarious and talented and uniting people!'

And then I look back towards the bar. An elderly couple smile at me. I smile back, and the lady squeezes her husband's hand. They are clearly affected by the music. I feel proud that my friend – *my* friend! – is doing this. He finishes the tune. I start to stand up to welcome him back but he begins another one and so I sit down again.

I wonder when he will stop playing the piano? I think, though this thought disappears when I notice more people smiling at me and raising their glasses. And then I realise. These people assume we are a *couple*. Why *wouldn't* they? We are two men in a hotel drinking red wine and playing romantic songs to one another. Of *course* we are a couple. I go slightly red, and look over at David, just as he turns to me and smiles, broadly. Suddenly, David's little hat and silk scarf don't look quite so rock and roll. Suddenly, David's little hat and silk scarf look a little camp. I look around the bar again and on the sofas and chairs and in the corners and recesses are beaming faces, all trained on me.

What a lovely moment for him, they all seem to be thinking. Maybe it's their anniversary!

A lady leans in to me as she passes.

'He's *very* talented,' she says, and I say, '*Thank* you!'

Thank you? I kick myself. Why did I say *thank* you? Why didn't I say, 'Yes, he is'? By saying '*thank* you' I have just accepted the compliment for *myself*! By saying '*thank* you', I have taken on the implied role of doting lover! I am his wife!

As a proud metrosexual and fervent anti-homophobe, I feel I should simply ignore any and all awkwardness, but it's hard, because David's started *yet another* romantic ditty, and he's just glanced back at me and smiled again.

Why does he keep playing romantic ditties? I think, panicking, but disgusted with myself for caring. And why does he keep glancing back at me while he's playing them? Have I fundamentally misunderstood what's going on here?

He finishes his tune, and for a horrible moment I think he is going to start another one – perhaps 'Daniel' by Elton John, or 'It's Raining Men' – but he stands up to a smattering of polite applause and sits next to me. I high-five him in as manly a way as I can muster.

'My wife enjoys piano music!' I say, quite loudly.

'I'm Bonnie,' says a girl, suddenly there next to us. It's the one who was watching at the start. 'I enjoyed your music.'

'Thank you,' says David. 'Do you play?'

'A little,' she says.

And then they walk off to the piano and play Chopsticks together.

David glances over at me and winks. This is what he'd been aiming for all along. I should laugh and give him a blokey thumbs-up, but instead I scowl as I jealously watch them duet.

That harlot, I think. He was *mine*.

THE STRANGER

xchanging smiles with strangers is one of the small pleasures in life. When it starts to go wrong, however, is when they *keep* smiling at you.

I'd noticed the man smiling at me almost as soon as I'd got through to Colin, on the phone. I'd smiled back, of course, because it would have been rude not to, and I am not a rude man. Politeness is *important*.

But then the man had raised his eyebrows at me and waved. And it suddenly struck me: this man thought he *knew* me.

There is nothing worse than not remembering someone, especially when they're raising their eyebrows at you and waving. And so I raised my own eyebrows, and I waved back at the man.

'You're not even listening to me,' said my friend Colin, on the other end of the phone.

'I am!' I said. 'But I'm waving as well.'

'At who?'

I shrugged. Which was pointless, really, because Colin was in his flat, and as such couldn't quite make me out.

I'd been talking to Colin about his advice of the week before. *Sensible* advice: Get a will. Because you never know. It could happen to you.

Surely, I'd thought, this was the kind of advice you gave to a *man*, not a *boy*. This was the kind of advice you gave to people who own *gardening* equipment and stay *in* on Saturday nights! Not to people like *me*!

And then I realised that *actually*, I own a Flymo, and *actually*, what I usually do on Saturday nights is watch *The Weakest Link* and eat a samosa.

And so I'd traipsed off to an office near Wembley and had a man do my will.

'You can't just stand there waving at strangers,' said Colin.

'I've stopped waving now,' I said. 'Now I'm just raising my eyebrows and smiling at him.'

'What's he doing?'

'He's raising his eyebrows and smiling at *me*. He *definitely* thinks he knows me.'

Perhaps, I thought, this was down to telly. I sometimes pop up on there, and for a few days afterwards I'm approached by people who sort of think they might know who I am, but inevitably don't.

'Excuse me,' a girl had said to me the week before, in a pub. 'Are you Danny Glover?'

I wasn't sure what to say.

'Danny *Glover*?' I'd said. 'You mean the black actor from the *Lethal Weapon* films?'

'Yes,' she'd said. 'Will you sign this? To Emily.'

She handed me a piece of paper. I wanted to tell her I wasn't Danny Glover, that I never *had* been, but I could see in her eyes that she really *wanted* me to be Danny Glover, and so politeness prevailed. I took her pen and wrote: 'To Emily, from Danny Glover, the black actor from the *Lethal Weapon* films.'

And she looked at it. And she said, 'Thanks!'

So maybe *that* was it.

'Maybe he thinks I'm Danny Glover,' I said, and then, because I felt I was being rude to the man, I pointed at the phone, rolled my eyes, and mouthed the word 'Sorry!'

'I'm going to have to walk away,' I said. 'He's just standing there ...'

And then, as I'd started to move away, the man pointed at the pub behind him and mouthed the word … 'Pint?'

And because I didn't know what else to do, I nodded. *Gah.* The man gave a double thumbs-up and dashed inside.

'You can't go for a drink with him!' said Colin. 'You don't even know his *name*!'

'I have to be *polite*,' I said. 'Politeness is *important.*'

And then I closed my eyes, hung up, and walked into the pub.

'So – how've you been?' said the man, handing me my pint.

'Oh gosh,' I said. 'I'm good! Yes. You?'

'Yes! You know me …'

I just smiled, because actually, I didn't.

'And how's … work?' I said. Oh God. What if he didn't *have* a … work?

'Well, you can imagine,' he said. 'Not the happiest job in the world!'

He laughed a lot at this, and because I didn't know what else to do, I did too.

Why can't I just tell this bloke I have no idea who he is? I thought. *Why did I have to be polite?*

'So, I was just trying to think … when was the last time I saw you?'

It was a *brilliant* piece of strategy. If we *had* met before – if this man *did* know me – I'd be able to start to place him …

'Tuesday,' he said, confused.

Tuesday?!, I thought, confused.

'Yeah, no, *obviously* Tuesday. I mean, *before* Tuesday. When did we meet before Tuesday?'

'We'd *never* met before Tuesday,' he said, slowly.

'Yeah,' I said, inexplicably.

'I'm the bloke who did your will,' he explained.

'I *know*!' I said, hoping to convince him I'd known all along. 'My *gosh* …'

'Who did you *think* I was?'

I took a sip of my pint.

'I thought you might think I was Danny Glover.'

I decided, later, I was glad I had my will sorted, and that maybe I should stop being so polite.

Because, in the words of the black actor from the *Lethal Weapons* films, I was getting too old for this shit.

COCAINE

I have overslept. Right now, right this very second, I am supposed to be in the lobby of a swanky London hotel waiting for an American man to come down from his room so we can have breakfast together.

It is a breakfast meeting – something as alien to me as a paintball lunch or a judo picnic – and I leap out of bed and run to the bathroom to frantically take stock of myself. It's not great news. I look surprised and messy. This T-shirt will do, I think. I pull my jeans on, smear some wax in my hair and call the cab company down the street. I throw my toothbrush at the sink, grab a jacket, and nineteen minutes later I'm stumbling, bleary-eyed but minty-mouthed, through the doors of the hotel.

'Hey, I'm so sorry I'm late,' I say, finding the American man at his table, having just finished another meeting.

'*I* came all the way from *New York* and *I* was here on time!' he says.

I laugh at his joke, which I realise is funny because *he* only had to come *downstairs* whereas *I* had to come a lot *further*, and then I wonder whether I should explain why it is funny, but then realise that is why he said it in the first place, and so I just keep laughing.

'So you were out partying last night?' he says. 'I know what you guys are like over here ...' I laugh again, but I *wasn't* out partying last night. I was *in* last night, watching *Celebrity Masterchef* and eating a Nando's.

'Yeah,' I say, gratefully accepting his lifeline, and noticing just how nicely turned out and well groomed he is. 'It was a … thing. Some big thing I went to. It was… in London.'

He nods his neatly combed head of hair, willing further information from me.

'And I had a Nando's.'

He seems bemused, but it's enough. He claps his hands together and starts the meeting, but then a waiter is by our side.

'Oh … sure, let's order,' says the American. 'I know what I'm having, how about you?'

'Um … anything's fine,' I say, not wanting to be a burden, but when you've got a waiter there it's not really an acceptable answer.

The American graciously looks at his menu to take the pressure off me, and I'm just saying 'Bacon and eggs, please' when I notice the waiter raising his eyebrows at me and then flicking his top lip with his index finger.

Oh, God. It is the international sign for 'there's something coming out of your nose'. Oh my *God*. There is *something coming out of my nose*. There is something coming out of my nose *at a meeting with an important and well-groomed American*. One I was *late* for. One I'm wearing *last night's clothes* for.

I nod a quick thank you to the waiter and self-consciously bat at my nostrils just as the American looks back up.

'And I'll have the same,' he says, folding his menu and handing it away.

The waiter leaves and I lean forward on to the table, affecting a look of seriousness but actually just covering my nose with my fingers. The American looks a little uncomfortable. It is a very small table and our faces are now a little too close together. I lean back but maintain the same dynamic with my arms and hands. The American relaxes and continues.

'So I think this project has great potential,' he says, and I nod, vigorously, all the while squeezing at the bottom of my nose with my fingers and sniffing. I can't feel anything. Maybe whatever it was has gone. But I can't take any chances. I stop squeezing but give it a couple of casual brushes with the back of my hand and one deep sniff.

'… and with the right kind of backing, it could really …'

God. What if through my batting and squeezing and sniffing and brushing I've actually *dislodged* whatever was there? What if it's no longer coming out of my nose? What if it's *out*? I'm nodding madly, but I'm not listening to the American at all. I'm worrying about where on earth this thing has gone. What if it's on my lips, or on the end of my nose? My God! My *nose*! What if it's on my *nose*?

I lean forward again and cover my nose. I know I am moving around too much but this is damage limitation. The American man looks a little startled but continues talking, now leaning back in his chair a little as he does so. I bat once again at my nose and try to hide it with more vigorous nodding. He says something that sounds like it might be a joke and I laugh loudly. Turns out it wasn't a joke.

And then some words ring through my head.

'*I know what you guys are like over here …*'

Suddenly, I realise exactly what I look like. The American has started to avoid my eye but I *know* what I look like.

I look like I am on drugs. I am laughing and fidgeting and sniffing and *I look like I am on drugs*!

I am not on cocaine! I want to shout. But doing so would just make me look paranoid, and surely *that* would be just more 'evidence'?

And so I accept the inevitable. That he will have to see that something has come out of my nose. I sigh, and I lean back, and I start to listen to what he has to say.

Half an hour later, I am in the toilets of the hotel. I look in the mirror. There is nothing coming out of my nose. There is, however, a big, white, minty ring of toothpaste around my mouth. I realise what the waiter had been trying to tell me.

The American thought he knew what we're like over here, but even *he* must have been surprised to learn that we all seem to *eat* cocaine before breakfast. I only hope he doesn't now think that's what 'I had a Nando's' means.

I wash my face.

LIES

I am caught off guard by a question I didn't see coming.

'You still on for tomorrow?'

'Tomorrow?' I ask.

'Yeah – my birthday?'

Oh, blimey. Tomorrow? Tom's birthday? But I'm so tired! I want to sit around in my pants and watch bad TV! I'd *planned* it!

'Ah!' I say, trying to buy time.

'Ah?' he says.

'I'm so sorry – I meant to tell you – I'm not going to be able to make it!'

I make a sorry face and shrug. Tom has always been cool about these things. Always the first to say, 'Hey, no worries – next time!' But what I see before me is a *new* Tom. A Tom who looks at me with hurt and soulful eyes.

'Why?' he says, pained.

Just say you'll go, I think. *Look at him!* But it is too late. I'm in too deep. I've said I can't. And so I say …

'I'm actually going to be in Turkey.'

Tom just stares at me.

'*Turkey?*' says Colin, in the pub, later that night. 'Why did you tell him you were going to Turkey?'

'I panicked!' I say. 'He looked so hurt! I had to make it good!'

'But … Turkey? Couldn't you have just said your parents were visiting? Or that you had some work to finish?'

I think about it. That would have worked, yes.

'Have you ever even *been* to Turkey? Where did you say you were going in Turkey?'

'The capital,' I say.

'Which is?'

'That's what he asked, and I couldn't remember, so I said it was actually just outside the capital – a village about an hour away that I couldn't really pronounce.'

'And what did you say you were doing in this village about an hour from the capital of Turkey?'

'I said it was an impulse buy. That my wife had always wanted to go to this village an hour outside of the capital of Turkey.'

'Who goes on impulse trips to villages about an hour away from the capital of Turkey? He'll know you're lying!'

'I know! But once I'd started, he just kept looking all hurt, so I had to embellish! I said they make these little silver thimbles there that she wanted to buy for her mum!'

'So her mum collects little silver Turkish thimbles? And you have to collect them in person? You have to remember that for the rest of your life! Whenever Tom's around you'll have to mention little silver thimbles! Where are you flying from?'

'Eh?'

'Where are you flying from? You need to know the details!'

Oh, God. Colin is right. What if Tom starts asking me questions? What if he wants to see photos? What if I am not 100 per cent up to speed with the intricacies of Turkish travel the next time I see him? I'm supposed to be leaving in the morning!

That night, I do some research. I see that from Gatwick I'd get to Ankara, which is the capital, having replaced Istanbul, which is actually bigger and used to be Constantinople. I see the country thrived in the Bronze Age, although there's no mention of silver, or thimbles, and I find that to get to a village an hour away, I would have to have got a transport service from the international terminal to the main bus terminal in town, which would have taken sixty minutes, before finding a train, the ticket for which would be about £3, or 6 lira.

My phone suddenly rings. I'm frightened. What if it's Tom, checking to see if my phone has an international ringtone yet? I am relieved to find it's my mum, who's phoned to tell me a story about someone I don't know doing something I don't understand. But I'm shaken.

'You can't lie in this day and age,' says Colin, on the phone, later. 'One ill-thought-out Tweet. One errant status update. You have to go dark. Turn your phone off. Close your blinds. You're taking a *big* risk.'

I find it hard to sleep that night. I look at my wife resting peacefully beside me. What dark world of secrets and deceit have I brought her into? What dangers and troubles has my ruthless ambitions to stay in and watch telly in my pants brought to her? How will she react when I tell her we have to live a lie together – a lie which dictates we must forever refer to little silver thimbles from very specific areas of a country we've never been to?

I am just like Tom Cruise in a Tom Cruise film.

The next day, I cancel my trip, and I go to Tom's party instead.

It's fun.

POTATOES

There is almost nothing that annoys me about my wife. Nothing, apart from the fact that every meal she eats – no matter how small – will always end up with me staring at her plate, shaking my head.

Tonight, it has happened again. She has left a tiny piece of potato on her plate. Everything else has gone. Only the tiny piece of potato remains. She's put her knife and fork down next to it and given up. Given up, on Britain's smallest piece of potato. Sometimes, it's not potato. It can be anything. A hint of sausage. A mention of spinach. A rumour of cheese. But tonight it's potato.

Silently, I take the plates to the kitchen while she continues to watch *The X Factor*.

Now I will have to scrape that small piece of potato into the bin, I think. Am I not busy enough? Why could she not have eaten it? It's just a tiny piece of potato!

I risk it.

'Do you want this piece of potato?' I call out.

'No thanks,' she shouts, from the sofa. 'I'm full.'

I stare at the tiny piece of potato.

Full? I think. No one can be *that* full! It's the size of three peanuts! Even Morph would ask for seconds!

It would be better if this were some kind of eating disorder, but it isn't – it's something she read in a magazine about leaving the last bite. I quell my annoyance and sit back down to watch *The X Factor*. Dannii Minogue is telling someone they really made that song their own.

I cannot concentrate.

'In some cultures,' I say, curtly, 'it is *rude* to leave bits of your food lying about. It means you don't like it.'

'In other cultures,' she says, calmly, 'it is rude to eat everything on your plate, as it implies you have not been given enough.'

'Well, neither of those are our cultures,' I say. 'Or are you saying I have offended your culture?'

'No, you have not offended the Australian culture,' she says, and I have to stop myself saying something racist.

A moment passes.

'Whenever you bring me toast,' I say, 'there is always a bite missing. Perhaps if the "mouse" you sometimes blame this on weren't *quite* so hungry, it would be able to eat tiny bits of potato left on your plate.'

There is a pause.

'That's not really a mouse,' she says. 'It's me.'

I knew it.

But I decide to leave things there. I have *made* my point.

Two nights later, we are at a very posh restaurant. The food has been incredible, and we've laughed and laughed. I've cleared my plate of extravagant South Indian food and she's pretty much finished hers, apart from a lonely prawn sitting atop a tiny stamp of rice. Soon, the waiter is upon us. He picks up my dish, and then goes for my wife's, but stops … 'I'm so sorry,' he says. 'I thought you'd finished.'

'I had!' says my wife, smiling.

'But –' He turns to me and raises his eyebrows before turning back '– you still have one or two prawns left!'

He smiles, as if there's been a terrible mistake he's trying to make easier, and waits for our response. My wife looks to me for support.

And I smile at her.

Because this is what I've been *waiting* for. This is confirmation. *Independent confirmation!*

'Oh yes!' I say. 'There it is! Just a tiny prawn all on its own!'
I point at it. My wife widens her eyes.

'But I'm full,' she says, slowly.

The waiter and I share a glance. There is a very good chance I could come to love this man.

'The chef will want to know what's wrong with it,' he says, and I look at my wife and nod, and remember that in *some* cultures it's rude to leave things on your plate.

She starts to pick up her fork, and I realise, I could *do* this. I could *force* my wife to eat that prawn! *Force* her to abandon whatever magazine-madness is stopping her!

And as her fork gets closer to that prawn, I catch a look of defeat in her eyes, and it's enough to break my heart, and so I say, 'Actually, it was a wonderful meal, but we're both just really full up.'

The waiter says 'as you wish', and picks up the plates, and I resist the urge to mention the toast-mouse.

'I suppose we are just from different cultures, you and I,' I say, wisely. 'But we will make this work.'

We order dessert.

THE GIFT

am with my friend Steve in a local cafe when he says, 'Keep it a secret, but I've got Colin this *wicked* gift.'

'What is it?'

He tells me. It's a fancy cardigan we'd all seen in a style magazine. Colin had been particularly taken with it. He said it'd make him look like Hugh Jackman, which it would, unless you were looking at his face or body.

'That's a *wicked* gift!' I say, amazed. 'But expensive!'

'Our birthdays are coming up soon. He'll love it. Don't tell him, though.'

I shake my head and frown and say I won't. I am pleased to have been given such privileged information. I must be a very good person, to be trusted with information like this, I think.

A month later, Colin and I are at the pub. He is about to get up and leave. He's meeting Steve in an hour, for a joint birthday curry. But he appears to be going empty-handed. I panic. Tonight's the night Steve's going to give him his present!

'Colin, you can't go empty-handed,' I say.

'What?'

'You can't go empty-handed. Steve's ... got you a gift.'

'Steve's got me a gift?' says Colin. 'What sort of gift?'

'An expensive gift.'

I let the words hang in the air, and nod my head with great solemnity. It is clear no other details are necessary.

'How expensive? What is it?' asks Colin, who thinks they are.

'It's just expensive,' I say. 'All you need to know is it's expensive. And wicked.'

Colin considers my words and comes to the correct conclusion.

'I'd better get him something,' he says. 'A DVD?'

'More expensive.'

'Two DVDs?'

'This gift is a *great* gift,' I say, and eventually, Colin gets the idea. He thanks me, and I don't feel bad for warning him, because this way, everyone's a winner. Steve would want this to happen. Wow. I really *am* a good person, I think. And then I finish my pint and go home.

The next day, I get a phone call from Colin.

'Well, thanks a bunch,' he says. 'I spent nearly fifty quid on that box set.'

'So?' I say, amazed at Colin's ungrateful attitude. 'Steve spent more on *your* present!'

'Oh, did he?'

'Yes! A *lot* more! You're lucky to have a friend like Steve!'

'Oh, am I?'

'Yes!'

'So where *is* my present?'

'Eh?'

'We sat down for our curry, and then I said happy birthday and handed him my gift. And he opened it and looked delighted and said he *loves* Bruce Willis, and then he popped it in his bag and started studying the menu.'

I am stunned.

'So he didn't give you the gift?'

'No.'

'*Nothing*?'

'I am giftless. And nearly fifity quid down.'

'He was supposed to give you that cardigan!' I say. 'The one you said would make you look like Hugh Jackman!'

We fall into silence. Why has Steve done this? And how do I raise it with him? It's his right to not give someone a gift. But surely there's been some mistake? Some clerical error? Steve *knows* he told me! He was there when it happened! He *knows I'd know*! I have to say something.

The following night, we all agree to meet at the pub at the end of my road. Steve will try and get there on time, he says, but he's meeting an old friend first. Colin arrives early, and we hatch a plan.

'We have to raise it subtly,' I say. 'We can't be too obvious. You will look ungrateful and mean otherwise.'

'You got me into this,' he says, unkindly. 'You get me out of it.'

And then we look up. It's Steve.

'I brought Mike,' he says, and behind him, in the drizzle of a London night, we see a stranger, paying a taxi.

'Hello, Steve,' says Colin, icily. 'You're late.'

Steve sits down and casts me a quizzical glance. I try not to give the game away.

'So I hear Colin gave you a Bruce Willis box set!' I say, brightly, and something slowly dawns on him. His eyes dart nervously between us.

His friend walks in and takes his coat off.

Suddenly, he looks a lot like Hugh Jackman.

THE WISDOM AND PHILOSOPHIES OF A MODERN MAN: 1

MONDAY

I think a nice thing to do is to contradict demeaning graffiti. How horrible for someone named Jake, for example, to walk into a pub toilet and see the words 'Jake Smells!' written on the wall. Which is why I always write 'No he does not!' underneath something like this. It gives me a nice warm feeling inside. Although to achieve that nice warm feeling, I sometimes *also* have to write the words 'Jake Smells!' Still, I think karma-wise, things are pretty even, so who's complaining?

Just Jake, and that's rich, because he stinks.

TUESDAY

I bet a good way to keep people on their toes is to tell them you've got a special carpet which will electrocute their heels.

WEDNESDAY

I have started playing Xbox on-line. It is good, because you get to talk to all sorts of different people from around the world. Well, I say 'all sorts of different people'. You get to talk to nerds or very aggressive people. One of them tried to start a fight with me. 'You wouldn't mess with me if you saw me!' he shouted. 'I'm six foot six"!'

'Yeah?' I retaliated. 'Well, I'm six foot six and a half!'

'I weigh two hundred and forty pounds!' he shouted.

'I'm two hundred and forty-one pounds!' I yelled.

'Where do you live?' he shouted.

'North London!' I yelled back.

'Me too!' he said.

I switched the Xbox off and drew my curtains.

THURSDAY

You know what? If I had to decide whether I would be a dog with wings, or a cat who could talk, I would be the dog with wings, because if there were dogs with wings, that's all cats would talk about anyway, and surely it's better to be up there in the sky, having fun and being talked about, than a cat who just sits there, bitching?

That's what I think anyway. You probably have your own thoughts.

FRIDAY

My wife recently paid good money to adopt a puppy on my behalf. I now receive regular updates from a puppy who has some-how learnt to write and post letters herself. Her name is Joanna and she has, so far, sent me several pictures which demonstrate exactly how my wife's £5 a month has improved her life. In some of them, she is playing with a small colourful ball, which I like to think we have provided.

All was well, until I was round at my mate's flat, and saw a picture of a familiar-looking dog sellotaped to his fridge.

'How do you know this dog?' I demanded.

Turns out Joanna has been spreading it around, the little bitch. I doubt she even *wrote* those letters.

SATURDAY

I think a good thing to do if you are stuck in the roleplay section of a job interview is to shout 'BEAR!' and pretend a giant bear has just stormed into the office. This will not only distract the interviewer, but also show them how you would deal with the crisis of a bear storming into their office, and when they're deciding on who to give the job to, you will definitely have made an impression, because who wants a bear storming into their office when there's no one to deal with it?

You can also do this with birds, if the office is a small one.

SUNDAY

My granddad used to say that it is good to reach out and touch people, but ultimately it was just that attitude that led to his arrest.

SUMMER

THE GATECRASH

I am throwing a small summer party in a fancy bar with my friend, Paul. We have rented a room, created a guest list, bought some champagne, and ordered some canapés. We are excited.

And then our friends and loved ones start to arrive. His friends congregate on one side of the room. My friends congregate on another. Gradually, as the champagne flows, they begin to intermingle.

I turn to see an impressed-looking Colin.

'Hey, what's GMTV's Richard Arnold doing here?' he asks. 'Is he a friend of yours?'

I frown, confused.

'GMTV's Richard Arnold?' I say. '*Where?*'

'*There!*'

Colin points at a man sitting at a table in the corner. It is indeed GMTV's Richard Arnold. What on earth is GMTV's Richard Arnold doing here?

'Well, that's strange,' I say. 'I don't remember Paul saying he knew GMTV's Richard Arnold. Perhaps he's here to do a soap update, or offer some opinions on this week's *Animal Park*.'

I shrug, and decide to ignore it, but I am secretly pleased. After all, GMTV's Richard Arnold has made the effort to turn up, and he has brought with him all the glitz and glamour of early-morning television. This, I realise, makes the party look *good*. It is now, thanks to GMTV's Richard Arnold, London's hottest minor-celebrity-based party. Every now and again, I cast a glance to the table in the corner, which now has some of our canapés on it, and I make sure that he is having a good time. He is laughing at something another stranger has said, and rocking his head back and forth.

Paul's a dark horse, I think, shaking my head. Inviting GMTV's Richard Arnold without telling me!

And then Paul is upon me.

'Your mate just blanked me,' he says.

'*Which* mate?' I say, appalled. It would not be like one of my friends to blank anyone – even Paul, who is a bit drunk and has mayonnaise on his lip.

'GMTV's Richard Arnold,' he says. 'He *blanked* me.'

'GMTV's Richard Arnold blanked you?' I say. 'But he's not *my* mate. He's *yours*!'

'*I* didn't invite GMTV's Richard Arnold. *You* must've.'

I cast my mind back. *Had* I invited GMTV's Richard Arnold? I did not *remember* inviting GMTV's Richard Arnold. But what if I *had*? Who *else* might I have invited that I had never before met and do not in fact know? What if Sian Lloyd turned up next? Or Lee Mead?

We both turn and stare at GMTV's Richard Arnold. He is eating a chip.

'What are we going to do?' I say, suddenly panicked. 'GMTV's Richard Arnold has turned up to our private party and is eating a chip!'

'We'll have to ask him to leave,' says Paul.

'We can't ask him to leave! He's a minor celebrity! You can't ask minor celebrities to leave private parties! There are *rules*! He must've made a mistake! We're in a central London hotspot! Minor celebrities are probably so used to going to parties in central London hotspots that he saw this one and just joined in! Maybe he thinks this is the *Shrek* premiere!'

'That was about fifteen years ago.'

'Well, what now?' I say, now genuinely worried. 'We can't have GMTV's Richard Arnold thinking he can just turn up to our private functions and sit at a table eating a chip whenever he feels like it! What if he follows us home? What if he thinks he can just move in to one of our spare rooms, or drive about in our cars? What if he *steals our pets*?'

'I agree,' says Paul. 'It is an inadvertent gatecrash, but GMTV's Richard Arnold must be *stopped*.'

We turn and stare at GMTV's Richard Arnold. He is looking straight at us. We realise we are both pointing at him, and so we turn away and pretend to be talking about something else.

'I think we've got to just ride this out,' I say. 'How many chips has he had?'

'I think just the one.'

'We're going to have to write that chip off. We'll go halvsies.'

'What if he has another one?'

'Let's cross that bridge when we come to it.'

And then inspiration strikes.

'What if we start *hugging* everyone?' I say. 'If we start *hugging* everyone, Richard Arnold might think it's weird that everyone is hugging and realise that he is the only person here who doesn't know anyone to *hug*! He'll realise his error and might even offer to pay for the chip!'

Immediately, Paul and I start to hug people. We start with each other, and then work our way around the room, hugging our friends but never explaining why. It is both tiring and embarrassing. When we have finished, GMTV's Richard Arnold has vanished. I feel guilty, but it was for his own good, and anyway, chips don't buy themselves.

I return to my corner, to find Colin looking bemused.

'What's Lee Mead doing here?' he says.

I cast my eye to the bar. Lee Mead is there, sipping champagne. I have never met Lee Mead before in my life.

I hug Colin.

'What are you *doing*?' he says, horrified.

I shrug, and pick up a chip.

THE SNIFF

ometimes, as I am walking home at night, I have noticed that any man walking in the opposite direction to me will sniff slightly as they pass. Or they'll cough. Or they'll wipe their mouth with the back of their hand. Since I've started to notice it, I've started to notice it *every time* I pass a fellow man. It has become a little disconcerting.

'Watch this,' I'll say to a friend, in the dying light of a summer night. 'This man will sniff or cough just as he walks past us.'

And then the man will sniff or cough just as he walks past us, and I will win a pound.

Now, I'm pretty sure this can't be happening just to me. This cannot simply be an elaborate way for me to win one pound every time I leave the house. If it is, I'm not sure who arranged it or what they're getting out of it, but they *must* be operating on a loss.

So it's *definitely* something else. But what?

'It's evolution!' says Colin, with wild, excited eyes. 'Don't you see? It's *evolution*! Do they *look* at you while they sniff at you?'

'They don't sniff *at* me,' I say. 'They just sniff. While averting their eyes.'

'And do you hear them sniffing *before* you pass? Do you hear them sniffing *afterwards*?'

'No – it's always exactly *as* we pass.'

'Do *you* ever sniff?'

I think about it. I suppose I *do* sometimes. But mainly I pat my pockets or look at my watch.

Hey – why do I pat my pockets or look at my watch?

'You're an *animal*, Dan,' says Colin. 'You're behaving just as a monkey would!'

'What do you mean?'

'You have identified some kind of primal reaction. You *must* have!'

I feel momentarily proud of myself. Colin thinks I must have identified some kind of primal reaction!

Wait. What?

'The men that are passing you at night do not know you. But they do not want to show weakness in front of a stranger. They need to remain strong and indifferent in the face of any potential threat.'

I think about what Colin is saying. And then my brain starts to hurt and so I ask him to say it again.

'They want you to know they're not afraid of you, Dan, and they also want you to know they mean you no harm.'

'So they sniff?'

'Yes. So they sniff. Or in your case, you pat your pockets. It makes you look distracted, which makes sure they know that conflict is not on your mind. It's *subconscious*!'

I think about what Colin has said as I step into the brisk evening air and walk home. It makes perfect sense. Chimps sometimes perform elaborate acts of strength to display their power while stopping short of overt aggression. Cats sit at an angle to one another to show they mean no harm. Perhaps men sniff at each other on dark streets to communicate the same. Perhaps this is the secret to world peace we have all been looking for. Perhaps if we can just crack the Sniff Code we can crack *all crime and conflict*!

I begin to feel mildly excited. I wonder if this is indeed an important sociological, evolutionary theory I have come up with. Maybe the Wallace Sniff will be lauded and hailed as a masterpiece of modern scientific thinking. Perhaps at last I will be welcomed into the scientific community and celebrated. They might name university wings after me, and take a picture of me in a hat, holding a scroll. Bright, attractive students will sniff at me as I pass them in the street, as a gesture of respect and admiration.

Actually, that'd be annoying.

Nevertheless, I suppose that, really, it was only a matter of time before I came up with a theory this groundbreaking and important. The Wallace Sniff. I am great.

Up ahead, I notice a man walking towards me. He is bigger than me and muscular, and he's staring straight ahead.

Avoiding eye contact!, I think, in some kind of wise, scientific voice. This man is no threat to me!

Instinctively, though, my hand goes for my pocket. But I stop the pat halfway through. No, I think. Go for the sniff. The sniff is more respectful. The sniff is *universal*. The sniff will *end all wars*.

I am excited as we approach one another. I aim to show him I am distracted and not thinking of him as a potential enemy. The urge to pat my pocket and perhaps hum a tune is strong, but I must ignore it. And then the man is just a few feet away, and I'm *sure* he's about to Wallace Sniff, but he *doesn't* Wallace Sniff, and so I take a deep breath and …

I sniff loudly.

It is *brilliant*.

But he has not sniffed. He has not sniffed! He could be a *threat*! This is *terrible*! The theory has crashed, *and* I'm going to get beaten up by a big man!

And then … just a second later, and from somewhere a *moment* behind me … the big man sniffs back.

I smile broadly as I walk on, happy to have successfully avoided conflict. I am the new David Attenborough.

I award myself a pound.

SATAN

I have been made a godfather.

It is the most responsibility I have ever been given, and at first it frightened me.

'I'm going to have to renounce Satan!' I said, in a panic, to my wife, who has in an *extraordinary* coincidence been made godmother to the *very same* child. 'That's what they make you do! I'm going to have to stand up *in a church* and *renounce* him!'

'That's OK,' said my wife. 'You've never been a *massive* fan of his.'

'That's true,' I said. 'I think he's silly. But what if he takes umbrage? You can't expect to renounce Satan and not have him take umbrage! He is *notoriously* grumpy!'

'You could cross your fingers,' said my wife, and that made me feel a lot better.

But I bravely went through with it, and so far, life as a godfather has been relatively painless. According to Wikipedia, I am now supposed to be responsible for ensuring that my goddaughter's religious education is carried out, but as yet she seems uninterested in learning psalms, and prefers instead to shout. I have taken the decision to allow this to continue, mainly because I prefer to shout too, and it is important that if shouting is how she intends to live her life, she has a good role model to learn from.

And then I made a mistake.

'We'll pop round to yours on Sunday!' said the e-mail.

'Great! I'll bake a cake!' I cheerily replied, hitting Send before

I could truly consider whether my words would be taken in the jokey manner in which they were intended.

Moments later, a new e-mail arrived.

'I've just told Poppy that her godfather is going to bake a cake!' it read. 'She is *incredibly* excited. How lovely of you to make such an effort for her!'

I thought about replying, and saying, Woah there, chicken-lips, there's been a *terrible* misunderstanding, but within a minute I'd received a photo of an almost unbearably happy child, her eyes all lit up like she'd swallowed a torch and inexplicably coughed it up into her head.

'She's been jumping around since she heard the news!' read the message.

I broke into a sweat. I can't cook. I'm awful. And then I remember: Fairy Cakes! Of course! They're supposed to be *easy*, aren't they? And kids *love* them!

'No,' says my wife, that evening. 'You can't make Fairy Cakes. You need to make a *proper* cake. For this is the world you have entered now.'

She's right. Poppy's parents are food *professionals*! He's a TV chef – she's a food photographer! Making Fairy Cakes for their child would be a sharp slap in the face of all that they stand for. It is the childish option. It is not something that a godfather would do. But how do I do it? How do I cook a cake for a small child? Do I have the right pans? How long do I boil it?

'Colin, how do you cook a cake?'

It was the same night and Colin had agreed to meet me for an emergency pint.

'Why do you need to know?' he asked. 'You can get them in shops. Or make Fairy Cakes.'

'I need to make my own,' I said. 'They will *know* if I don't. It would be a sharp slap in the face of all that they stand for. I need to show *responsibility*! I'm a godfather! And I've promised a small child!'

'You need an egg, I think,' said Colin, tapping his chin. 'And you cook it with that. You break it up and then you whisk it and then you have a cake.'

'There must be more to it than that,' I said, confused.

'Breadcrumbs,' said Colin. 'You put breadcrumbs on it and that makes it into a cake.'

'That's a Scotch egg you're describing! I can't give her a Scotch egg!'

'Put a candle on it. Or sprinkles. You can put sprinkles on anything and they'll love it. Put some sprinkles on an egg, she won't know the difference. That's what *I'd* do.'

Colin once worked for the Citizens Advice Bureau.

'Where do you get sprinkles?' I asked, now panicked. Colin shrugged. 'I think you can only get them on-line.'

On the way home, I bought some sprinkles from the newsagent on the corner, and studied them as I walked. This small and colourful tub now represented a new and frightening me. A grown-up me. A me of responsibility. Accountability. A me you can trust. A me who would offer to bake your child a cake, and then go out and buy some sprinkles so it would taste less bad.

Perhaps, I considered, this means I am growing up. Perhaps this small and simple gesture has been waiting inside me for years, biding its time, preparing to come out, gestating and refining itself. Perhaps subconsciously, I have been *needing* to make a cake for a small child and then buy some sprinkles from a Happy Shopper.

I can *do* this. For *I* am a *godfather*!

It is an hour before they arrive, and I have burnt the Fairy Cakes. I have tried to mask the burnt bits with sprinkles but the tub the newsagents sold me was out of date and they have expanded and congealed.

I consider the Scotch egg at the back of the fridge, but I've run out of candles.

I kick myself.

'This is what happens when you renounce Satan,' I say, shaking my head.

PYJAMAS

I am embarrassed because my wife has caught me.

'What are you *doing*?' she says, moments after walking into the bedroom. She looks *horrified*. I had hoped she wouldn't notice, that perhaps I could get away with this.

'I can explain!' I yell, desperately, but it is too late. She has seen me. She takes her wide eyes and walks into the bathroom, possibly to sit down, and shake a bit.

I am wearing little pyjamas.

I didn't mean to. It just happened.

I'd just returned from a few weeks away on the other side of the world, working. It had been a tough routine of constant flights, drab and dusty hotels, punishing early mornings and very late nights. Of long car journeys and bad fast food. Of throat-drying air conditioners and bone-chilling winds. But in the middle of it all … I found *comfort*. Comfort in the form of a free pair of slightly undersized cotton airline pyjamas. Pyjamas that I only put on, that first, fateful night, because I was a shallow, jetlagged husk of a man, who stank of airplane and taxi and smog. I wasn't thinking straight. I was *confused*.

But everything changed in that one moment.

These pyjamas felt *good*. They felt … *right*.

Yes, they were a little too small, but that night, I slept the sleep of the innocent. I was warm. Comforted. Protected. I was a tiny cotton ball, all wrapped up in a charcoal sleep suit, and as my eyes opened the next morning, I realised … *my eyes had been opened.*

Pyjamas are *incredible*, I thought to myself. Why don't I *always* wear pyjamas?

I wanted to scream it to the world! *I am Danny Wallace, and I love wearing little pyjamas!* I wanted to text my friends! To ask them whether they, too, had discovered the delights of little pyjamas! To tell them there is *no need* to explain, that we could embark upon this journey together – that we could wear our little pyjamas with pride! Maybe it would just take *me* to show them!

But this, of course, was all through the freedom that travel brings. I was in a different country, in a different time zone. Anything seemed possible. The world was my oyster, and I would be *in* that oyster – a small and simple pearl bouncing happily around in a pair of cotton PJs.

As the trip had come to an end, however, a certain hollowness had begun to creep in. Because I knew that, for me at least, the world of pyjamas was soon to be over.

But why? I thought to myself, as I pretended to watch *Desperate Housewives* with my wife. Why must I deny who I really am?

'Coming to bed?' she'd said, as the credits began to roll.

I nodded, silently, and then decided: tonight would be the night I'd test the waters. And twenty minutes later, I'm yelling, 'I can explain!'

'Look,' she says, the next morning. 'I don't mind if you want to wear pyjamas. I just wish you'd given me some warning. It was a bit of a shock.'

I am still wearing them and eating a bowl of Coco Pops.

'I'm so sorry,' I say. 'It won't happen again.'

But I know it will. Because I have become an *addict*. How could I have been blind to them all these years? Why had I not seen the signs earlier? My dad was virtually *born* in pyjamas. When did it become socially unacceptable for a man to wear formal night-wear? Have pyjamas gone the way of pipes and monocles? I'd look *great*, all dressed up in my pyjamas with a pipe and a couple of monocles! We *all* would! Why, then, do they bring such shame upon us? Why do our womenfolk frown upon us so? Maybe they just need to *see* us in our pyjamas to realise the comfort, the joy, the pleasure they bring! Maybe they will want their *own*. And if they do, we should be *kind*. We should simply pat them, patronisingly, on their heads, and say, 'There is no need to explain.'

I keep my pyjamas on all day. It is my own kind of protest. *Maybe this is what I will do*, I think, as I wander around the house, liberated. *Maybe I will wear pyjamas during the day, and change into more appropriate clothing when she gets home.* But I resent having to go underground with this.

At half past six, though, I get changed into jeans and a T-shirt.

My wife is a little late home. *Perhaps she's stopped off for a drink with her friends*, I think. *To come to terms with things. Settle her nerves. I've come out of the closet, wearing a little pair of pyjamas, after all, and this kind of thing can have an effect on the unenlightened.*

When she arrives home, things are a little stilted.

'Hello,' I say.

'Hello,' she says.

She puts her bags down and gives me a kiss on the cheek.

'I just got a couple of microwave meals from M&S,' she says. 'Is that OK?'

'That's great,' I say.

There's an awkward moment.

I look in the bag.

She's bought herself a little pair of pyjamas.

'I can explain!' she says.

'There is no need,' I say, patting her on the head. 'There is no need.'

HEROES

am sitting outside a cafe in the sun with my friend Rich when we spot a giant, lolloping man harassing strangers. He is sidling up to them and then shouting in their faces, madly. Rich and I stare deep into our coffees, hoping for all the world that we're not next on his agenda of shouting and madness.

Now the man is giggling insanely and swatting imaginary flies away from his face, as he bothers an elderly woman drinking tea on her own. He sits down next to her and begins to rant about Tibet, just inches from her face. She stands and leaves.

'That poor woman,' I say. 'We could have saved her from that man.'

'Yes,' replies Rich. 'We could have been heroes!'

We watch the man pacing around, looking for someone else to shout at. Two French students with backpacks and maps approach and take a seat, oblivious to what's going on. The man homes in on them.

'Oh no!' I say. 'Rich! He's going for the French!'

The man begins shouting in their faces.

'There's no such thing as a free lunch!' he's shouting, laughing almost uncontrollably after each time he says it. 'There's no such thing as a free lunch, is there?'

'This is terrible, Rich,' I say. 'Imagine the impression these poor students will get of our proud and noble country! They will think we consist only of shouting men who wander around dashing all hopes of free lunches!'

'We should intervene,' says Rich. 'But how do we do it without attracting his attentions ourselves? I don't want to spend ninety minutes learning that there's no such thing as a free lunch.'

Now the man is doing squat-thrusts in front of the students. He jumps to his feet, and shouts, 'See? *Exercise!*' The students don't really know how to react, and smile politely. They clearly need to escape. But *how?*

'Quick!' I say. 'I've got an idea! We can offer them an out!'

'How do you mean?' says Rich.

'I mean, *you* speak a bit of French! You could go inside, go to the toilet, and then come out again as if you're part of their group! You could tell them they're welcome to join us over here! It would be like *code!*'

'Yes,' says Rich. 'That's an excellent plan. We will be heroes!'

'Heroes!' I say, and we clink our cups of coffee together.

Rich leaves it a moment, and then gets up to go.

'All I need to do is look confident and talk loudly,' he says. 'Wish me luck!'

'*Bon chance!*' I say, and in he goes.

This will be great, I think to myself. It will be an important moment. A chance to show that not all Brits are as loud and odd as this man. That these Frenchmen are welcome here. That we are polite enough to know their language, and will use it to rescue our European brothers. *We are heroes*, I think.

I shake my head, softly, as I watch the man do more squat-thrusts in front of the now-terrified students, before he leaps up and shouts, 'THERE'S NO POPE IN THE VATICAN! THERE'S NO POPE IN THE VATICAN!'

Once again, he's inches from their faces, and the students glance nervously at each other, muttering something under their breath.

Worry not, my French friends, I think. *Help is at hand.*

But then I catch the tail end of what they're saying. And then I break out in a sweat. Because I've realised something awful. These students are *not* French. They're *Italian*.

I look through the window of the cafe, and see Rich swing the toilet door open and stride through the room, full of confidence and swagger. His eyes are fixed upon the students and there's a smile on his face.

'Wait!' I want to shout. 'Wait a second!'

But I can't shout that. And I can't catch his eye. Rich is a man on a mission. A heroic mission, to save the Italians he mistakenly thinks are French.

'THERE'S NO POPE IN THE VATICAN!' shouts the man, even louder this time. The students try to make their move.

And then Rich pushes the door open, hard. It swings and clatters against the wall. Everyone turns and looks at him. Rich has inadvertently blocked their exit. He opens his arms and grins an *enormous* grin.

'BONJOUR!' he shouts. 'MES AMIS! JE VOUDRAIS VOUS INVITER A BOIRE AVEC MOI ET MON AMI POUR ECHAPPER A LA FOLIE!'

The students look at him with sheer terror in their eyes.

'THERE'S NO POPE IN THE VATICAN!' shouts the madman behind them, trying to regain their attentions. But Rich is having *none* of it.

'VENEZ AVEC MOI MAINTENANT!' he yells. 'NOUS IRONS BIEN, VOUS ET MOI!'

For a moment, I think the Italians are going to cry.

Who are these people?, they seem to be thinking. What harm do they mean us?

Rich has stopped yelling. His smile falls. This hasn't worked as well as he'd hoped. The madman returns to his squat-thrusts.

'Rich,' I half-whisper. '*Rich!*'

The Italians turn their stunned gaze to me. Clearly, they think I'm now about to join in too, possibly with a few star jumps, or a new theory about the Pope.

'They're *Italian*, Rich!'

'Oh,' says Rich, and he turns to face them once more. '*Je suis desolée.*'

'Who's gonna get me a drink?' shouts the madman, inches from Rich.

The Italians smile politely and sneak off.

Rich and I spend ninety minutes learning that there's no such thing as a free lunch.

PUNCTUALITY

I was sitting on my own in a stranger's living room at a quarter past eight at night, with a small bowl of cashews on my lap, wishing I was somewhere else.

My friend Peter had invited me along that morning, saying his friend was having a house party and that everyone was welcome.

'OK!' I'd said, excitedly. 'What time?'

'Oh … eightish …' he'd said.

It was now 8.20 and I was still the only person there.

I could hear the stranger clattering away in the kitchen, moving bowls and getting canapés out of the oven. This didn't seem like a house party to me. This seemed more like a *dinner* party.

'Um … excuse me? Sandra?' I called out.

'It's Sandi,' she said, walking into the living room and looking severe.

'Oh. Hey, this isn't, like, a *dinner* party, is it? Only Pete told me it was a *house* party and I don't want to look like I've *gatecrashed* …'

'No …' she said, flatly. 'It's just a small party.'

She was right. At this point in time, it was the smallest party in Europe. I waited for her to reassure me that I was not a gatecrasher, but she must've forgotten.

'I'm moving jobs, y'see,' she said.

'Oh! Congratulations!' I said.

'Yeah, I was made redundant.'

'I'm very sorry.'

'But I'm glad I'm moving.'

'Good!'

'My last job was full of … *bullying*.'

'I'm very sorry.'

I *had* thought that by engaging my new host in friendly banter we might forge some kind of bond by the time any other guests arrived, but all it did was highlight just how little I knew about her. I tried to work with what I had around me.

'I see you've got a lot of Adam Sandler DVDs!' I said, pointing at a pile underneath her telly. 'You must really like Adam Sandler!'

'They're my ex-boyfriend's. He left recently and I've not had time to clear things up. Not with everything that's been going on with my mother.'

'No …' I said, closing my eyes and nodding sympathetically, 'Of *course* …'

I was hoping my silent, blind nodding would give the impression that I knew *exactly* what had been going on with her mother, but I think all it did was make me look a little simple. Inside, I was kicking myself. Why had I arrived at eightish? You should *never* arrive at eightish! Other people *hate* people who arrive at eightish! *I* don't. I usually think promptness is *much* undervalued. But only if you know the person whose house it is. If it's the house party of a strange woman who's lost her job and had trouble with her mother, you probably shouldn't arrive at all. Promptness is *rubbish*.

Why had I done this? Why had I forgotten to come late? Why hadn't Pete reminded me of the etiquette when he'd said, 'Yeah, just pick up a bottle of wine and head over about eightish …'?

Oh. Hang on.

Oh, God. I'd forgotten the wine, too.

I waited for Sandi to frostily leave the room, got my phone out, and texted Pete.

'*I forgot to bring wine and she hates me!*' I wrote, and a moment later, I got my reply.

'*Wow. You there already?*'

Yes! Of course I was! Because he'd told me to be! And yet this was still *my* fault! It's not like I hadn't held parties in the past and not been thrown by the early arrivals. A few years ago, I'd told people to turn up at my place at sevenish. By eight o'clock, the only people who'd turned up were a man, his baby, and Steve Strange from 80s new romantic band Visage. This was a surprise to me, as I did not know Steve Strange, and yet here he was, in full make-up, in my living room. When my friend Simon arrived a little while later, thinking the party might be in full swing, he found instead me, a baby, and Steve Strange, all sitting on a sofa. 'Well, I wasn't expecting *this*,' had never seemed a more appropriate comment.

And now *I* was that man. *I* was Steve Strange from 80s new romantic band Visage! And that's a sentence I never thought I'd write.

I sat there, praying for the doorbell to ring, but it mocked me with its silence. Sandi popped back into the room. She still had a testy air about her, despite my brilliant performance in our earlier conversation.

'What was your name again?' she said.

'Danny,' I said.

'Would you like another beer, Danny? They're a bit warm. They haven't really had the chance to cool down yet.'

I blushed. Even the *beers* had been surprised at how early I was.

And then – the blessed relief of the doorbell, and within twenty minutes, the place was buzzing. Even Peter had made it, with two bottles of wine.

'Why did you get here so early?' he said. 'You *never* turn up when you're told to … I'm going to have to apologise to Sandi …'

'But *you* told me what time! You should have told me to come *later*!'

'I'd been told *eightish*! So that's what I told *you*!'

I was about to point out how little sense this made, but Sandi was suddenly there, topping up our glasses.

'Sandi,' said Pete, 'listen, about Danny getting here at …'

But she ignored him, and turned to me.

'Danny, I just want to say that it was very good of you to arrive at eight o'clock, *as I had specified*.' She cast a stony eye at Pete. 'I think promptness is *much* undervalued.'

'As do I, Sandi,' I said, graciously. 'As do I.'

PASTRIES

I am in the huge, light, glass-and-metal foyer outside the office of a very important man. There are plasma screens everywhere and busy people rushing around, shaking their heads, and studying pieces of paper.

I sit quietly with a small cup of takeaway tea and a croissant.

'This is very different from *my* office,' I think, to myself. 'In *my* office there is just *me* and some unopened mail.'

I bite into my croissant and notice a homeless man outside. He is shuffling around, looking at his feet, and he glances inside. I stop chewing my croissant. It feels rude.

'Danny?'

I look up. It is the important man's assistant, who has come to collect me.

Imagine having an assistant! I think, as we walk through the building together. You'd be able to get all sorts of assistance with things. You could say, 'Quick! I need some assistance!' and be guaranteed to receive it. I bet *they* never have any unopened mail lying around the place. Maybe *I* should try and be important enough to have an assistant.

In every office we pass, there are more important people, being important, and being assisted by their assistants. I am jealous. Finally we arrive at the office of the important man I'm here to meet.

'Please do take a seat,' says the assistant. 'He'll be here in just a second. And help yourself to a pastry!'

She says this with joy in her voice and indicates a plate of them. She hovers by the door, waiting for me to take one, but I've just finished my croissant, and I don't really feel like another. She looks disappointed.

'I'll have one in a moment,' I promise, but the door has closed.

I stare at the pastries in silence.

The door opens and in strides the important man.

'Danny!' he says, and we shake hands. 'Have you had a pastry yet?'

'I haven't!' I say. 'I just finished one of my own.'

'Oh,' says the man. 'Well – have another one!'

'I'm fine,' I say, patting my tummy and making a satisfied face, to show that I am satisfied, and that I have a tummy.

'They're very *good* pastries,' says the man, raising his eyebrows and pushing the plate slightly towards me. 'Freshly made. Bought *especially* for this meeting!'

'Please don't let me stop you,' I say, generously. 'Do please feel free to eat one yourself!'

'Well, you first,' he says. 'I had quite a big breakfast!'

'Well, maybe *I'll* have one when *you* have one!' I say.

We are both being very jolly about things but it is clear that there is a certain tension growing. This is becoming some kind of pastry-off.

'Come on,' he says, picking up the plate. 'I *insist*.'

'I *really* couldn't,' I say, quite firmly, and holding up my hands.

There is an awkard moment. Suddenly, the important man's voice lowers. His eyes dart nervously towards the door.

'We've *got* to eat a pastry,' he says. 'We've *got* to. She went out to get these this morning. She went to a *lot* of trouble.'

I suddenly realise the seriousness of the situation. If we don't eat one, the important man will get into trouble. Hey – *I* might too!

'But I just *had* a croissant,' I whisper. 'Downstairs! Moments before coming up! I think she even saw me!'

'*I* had a full English,' he says, desperately. 'I'll be lucky if I can fit a *coffee* in. *Please!*'

Suddenly, by the frosted glass door, we hear the important man's assistant, shuffling about. We both fall silent and hold our breath. The important man puts his hand out, ready to grab a pastry if she decides to walk in. It is *absolutely terrifying*. It's like that bit out of *Jurassic Park*. We can see her shape through the glass. We hold our breath. For a horrible moment, it looks like she's reaching for the door handle, but then from somewhere on her side of the door a phone rings, and she stalks away. We breathe out.

'I might have to hide some in my desk,' says the important man, desperately. He suddenly seems a little less important than before.

'But we're grown men!' I want to shout. 'Grown men shouldn't need to hide pastries in a desk!' But I don't shout that. Instead, scared, I say, 'good idea', and decide to help him.

He stands and grabs two small pastries and tip-toes over to his desk, never taking his eyes off the door. While he does that, I wrap a croissant in some tissue and pop it in my bag, then do the same with a pain-au-chocolat. We break another pain-au-chocolat in two to make it look like it's been somehow devoured.

'Hey,' I say, 'turn the plate slightly to make it look like it's been constantly to-ing and fro-ing between us.'

'Yes! Good!' says the important man. 'How about crumbs?'

Silently, we sprinkle some crumbs over the table and on two plates. The important man scrunches up a napkin and tosses it on the floor. I carefully place a flake of pastry next to it, and then two more. We look around us.

'Perfect,' we say.

We have our meeting. When it's over, we flinch as his assistant strides into the office. She takes in the scene. Her face falls. It is one of devastation. It looks like we've been throwing foodstuffs at each other for an hour. She scans the room, trying to work out where her huge number of pastries have gone. All that remains is one small piece of Eccles cake. The important man and myself look at each other, guiltily, and we shake hands and quietly say goodbye.

I don't think I want an assistant, I think, as I leave the building. *It is too much like having a boss.*

I offer my pain-au-chocolat to the homeless man outside.

He declines.

THE SKIRT

have been minding my own business all morning and up until now it has been going well. I've undertaken various minor chores on the high street, and ticked them off my list of things to do with pleasure and aplomb. The sun is shining, the bees are buzzing, and all is well with the world.

Until I see her.

Just there, up ahead – a larger lady maybe thirty feet ahead of me, carrying a plastic bag, and mopping her brow as the sun beats down. Perhaps she too has been undertaking minor chores on the high street and ticking them off her own list of things to do. Perhaps she too has gleaned a certain self-satisfaction from minding her own business all morning, as the sun shone, and the bees buzzed, and all seemed well with the world.

But she does not know. She cannot see what I can see. And I have seen too much.

I panic, and start to look around to see if anyone else has noticed … perhaps if they have, we can share this burden and divide this responsibility.

But no one has. Only I have noticed. Only I have seen that this larger lady up ahead of me – this larger lady with her plastic bag and her sweaty brow – is exposing parts of her she really can't have realised she's exposing.

Her skirt's all hitched up! I think, breaking into a sweat of my own. Someone has to tell her that her skirt's all hitched up!

I do not know what has led to this lady's tricky predicament – there is no wind and I can't imagine this is now the fashion for larger ladies – and I remain the only person who seems to have noticed. But what can I do? Is a man allowed to comment on something like this? What if she thinks me a pervert? What if she thinks *I* somehow hitched her skirt up from a distance of thirty feet?

There is only one thing to do. I dial my wife.

'Quick, you have to help me!' I say. 'There is a lady up ahead of me whose skirt's all hitched up!'

There is a moment's silence and I wonder if I'm about to get told off for noticing a lady's hitched-up skirt.

'Remain calm,' says my wife, finally. 'How hitched up is it?'

'It's *fairly* hitched up,' I say. 'I'm not sure about the percentages.'

'OK,' she says. 'You're going to have to say something.'

'What? No! Can't *you* say something?'

'I'm not there,' she says.

I look around and she is right. She is *miles* away.

'Can't I just ignore it?' I say. 'I mean, I've told *you* – maybe that's enough?'

'Has anyone else noticed?' she says.

'Not yet!' I say. 'Hey! I could shout something!'

'No. But you have to say something before anyone else sees.'

'Come on! This is not a job for a man!' I plead. 'And anyway, gravity might intervene!'

'It's a hot day,' she says. 'Gravity will not intervene. You know what to do.'

And she hangs up.

Why today?, I think. I was just minding my own business!

And then, up ahead, the lady stops walking and sets her bag down. I am getting closer with every passing second, but still I have no plan. Does saying 'hitched up' sound too rude? Is it a skirt or a dress? I need to think quick!

Now I'm only ten feet away, and I see her mopping her brow once more, and in just three or four seconds I'll face the only moment I'll have to right this wrong and say whatever I can say to make this OK, but *what the hell is it?* ... and now it's too late, and so, as I pass her, I take a deep breath and just say ...

'Skiiiirt!'

And I stride on.

Immediately, I go red. *Skiiiirt?* Was that enough? That's the kind of thing people on day release say! *Skiiiirt!*

As I prepare to round a corner and break into a jog, I allow myself just one embarrassed moment to look back at the woman, to see if she's angry or confused or insulted, but as I do, we lock eyes, and she looks grateful, and mouths the words 'Thank you' at me.

I feel all warm.

I give her a confident nod back as she subtly sorts herself out, as if I'm *always* doing things like this and am *totally* comfortable with it.

I text my wife an update, and stride on, a man who can tick 'help a damsel in distress' off his things-to-do list, and secretly, one who's hoping he might encounter more large women with their skirts all hitched up.

SERVICES

t is late at night and I am hungry and alone on the motorway. I pull in at a service station and look up at the wonders that could make my world a better place. There's a Burger King. A cafe. An M&S. My stomach flips and growls in anticipation.

I could have a Whopper! I think. Or one of those cheese and onion toasties from the posh cafe! Perhaps a hoisin duck wrap with some of those crisps in tubes that *look* like Pringles but *aren't*!

The car park is full of other Friday-night travellers, each drawn here by the tawdry but seductive siren that is the motorway services. Steam rises from warm bonnets, and somewhere up ahead of me, a woman violently shakes a door that won't open properly.

They have *showers* here now, I think, distracting myself. *Showers!* I could have a *shower*! I could eat my Pringles in the shower, then dry off in the toilets under one of those loud air machines!

But I am only an hour from home, and it is probably a little gauche to have a shower in a service station. I mean, what am I? The Queen?

The lights and logos continue to beckon, and I follow them, in search of the magic they promise, and before too many more moments are up, I am standing by the stained chairs in the centre of the station. A chill wind whistles through the broken automatic doors, ruffling the collars of my fellow travellers, who sit, blank-eyed and coats-on, shovelling limp fries and damp onion rings past their strip-light-yellow lips.

The magic has gone.

I stand in a depressed, heads-down queue and look at the floor. It has seen better days. When you are saying a *floor* has seen better days, you're in trouble. But I must persevere, because I am hungry, and this is food, and some people in Africa don't even *have* service stations.

The man next to me seems as affected as I am by this. He turns and gives me a half-smile, and I half-smile back, and think about how sad it is that we have to split a smile. He orders his bacon double cheeseburger meal and stands to one side. I order mine, and immediately feel embarrassed because he must think I'm *copying* him, especially as I've even ordered Fanta just like him, and so I stand a short distance away and pretend I'm the only person in the world who's ever ordered a Fanta at a service station.

Our meals arrive simultaneously, and I can tell we are both weighing up the options. Do we eat here, with the Others, or do we eat in our cars?

I decide instantly to eat in my car, but it seems he has too, because we both start to walk for the doors. There is an awkward moment when we are both striding at exactly the same speed, side-by-side, Fantas in hand, and so I slow down, and pretend to find a leaflet about the RAC absolutely fascinating.

Minutes later, I throw my bacon double cheeseburger meal on to the passenger seat. I am alone with my food, and soon I will be home, smelling of fries and Fanta, but it is dark, and so I switch the inside light on, and I start to gorge myself on food. I turn on the radio, and swig my Fanta, and somehow the sugar is already in my veins, and so I go with the moment, and start to jig my head about as Heart belts out a Will Young song I have never heard before and will never hear again. I can see my own reflection in my windscreen, and I look *cool*, and I bite into my cheeseburger and see how many fries I can stick in my mouth at once.

And then the food is gone, and I sit alone in the car park, away from the Others, and I happily watch my reflection as I do a little burp.

'I am *ready*!' I say to myself, and I put the keys in the ignition, start the car, and turn the headlights on.

And then I see him. The man from earlier. The man with the cheeseburger.

He is sitting in the car right opposite me, eight feet away, looking embarrassed. He is all lit up, and trying not to seem self-conscious as he wipes the ketchup from his mouth.

I realise he has been watching me, as I jig about to Will Young, shoving fries into my face and smiling at myself as I do little burps.

I half-smile at him, and he half-smiles back, and I imagine we both think about how sad it is that we have to split a smile.

MEN

I t's already been quite an annoying day.

There are builders tramping about on our roof, and I'm on hold with the phone company, who've decided I'm not to use my mobile any more.

'You've been downloading *quite* a lot of e-mails!' they say, chirpily, when finally they answer.

'Yes,' I say. 'But only the ones I've been *sent*!'

We both enjoy a little chuckle.

'Well,' says the man, 'because you've downloaded some of them while you've been abroad, I'm afraid your bill is a little larger than normal!'

'Oh dear!' I say, cheerily. 'Oh well. What do I owe you?'

There's a pause.

'It's just over one thousand pounds for the month,' says the man.

I am slightly stunned. And my stomach turns. Because already I know it's hopeless to argue. They'll always win. That's what *happens*.

'A *thous–*?' I start, but then my wife walks into the room.

'That builder outside has just been rude to me!' she says, shocked.

Rude? Someone's been *rude*? Outside my *house*? To my *wife*?

I make an apologetic face and point at the phone but she continues.

'They knocked our aerial,' she says, wide-eyed, 'and so I asked one of them if he could get the boss for me so he could sort it out, and he just stared ...'

'He just *stared*?' I say.

'Yes! And then I asked him again, and this time he just said "no" and then walked off!'

'He said "no"?' I say, now as shocked as she is. 'And then walked off?'

'He said "no" and then walked *off*!' she says.

My heart sinks. This is terrible news. Terrible because it means there is the possibility I will now have to *do* something. But I'm a pacifist! A man who avoids conflict wherever and whenever possible! A situation like this, however – in which a man has been rude to *my* wife on *my* property on *my* watch – well … this calls for *action*.

'I'll call you back,' I say, to the man from the phone company.

'Sounds like you'd better!' he says, cheerily, and I hang up.

'So …' I say, trying to work out how brave I'm feeling, 'how big was this man?'

My wife just raises her eyebrows.

'What I *mean* is,' I say, 'where is this man?'

She beckons me to the window and slowly lifts one of the slats of the blind, and points a man out. He is leaning on my wall, smoking a roll-up and laughing with his mates. He's wearing a hard hat and he looks like he spits. What's more, he looks like he probably spits at *dogs*, and when he does, they fall over. He drops his roll-up in my front yard and he looks up. We make brief, star-tling eye contact.

'*Him*?' I say.

'No,' says my wife. 'The one next to him.'

There is a smaller man, and that's a good thing, but he's still got back-up. He's got his mates. I'm just a boy with a small wife builders are rude to. And it's not like they're *my* builders. They're builders sent by the council to buff our street up. They're maverick builders outside my control. I'm nothing to them!

And then I think of the thousand pounds the phone company wants to charge me because I – shock! – used my phone. And how they'll be working on their excuses already, about how foreign megabytes are more expensive than British ones, and how if I'd *looked* at page forty of the fine-print on the 3,000-page dossier I'd signed fifteen years ago, I'd *know* these things, and I puff my chest up, and I swing the door open, and I say, '*You* – I need a word …', and the builder looks at me, and he looks at his mates, and I separate him from the pack, and I stare him straight in the eye.

'This is my property. And she is my wife. And when you are on *my* property and talking to *my* wife, you will do so with *respect*.'

The builder is wide-eyed. His mates look stunned. I am more stunned, but I am in the *zone*.

I go for the kill.

'And that goes for *all* of you,' I snarl.

I turn back, and pass my wife on the steps, who looks scared and impressed, and I pass the biggest of the builders, who looks away, and I slam the door shut.

'Wow!' says my wife, as I slump to the stairs. I am shaking slightly, and my eyes have gone all big, but I have done it. I have done it!

'Get me the phone company,' I yell, and she runs off to fetch the phone.

Five minutes later, they let me off the thousand pounds.

Sometimes – just sometimes – it's great realising you're a Man.

WEIGHT

he problem, as I see it,' says Colin, opening the crisps, 'is that I've been putting on weight, for no discernible reason whatsoever. It is a mystery to me, and to those who know me.'

He takes a sip of his pint.

'And it's concerning, Dan. *Deeply* concerning. I used to be *lithe*. Do you remember when I was lithe?'

Colin has never been lithe. I nod anyway.

'*Man*, I was lithe. People would look at me, and think, Look at him – *he's* lithe. But now? I'll be honest. It happens not so much.'

'So what are you saying?'

'I'm saying I've decided to *do* something. To *act*. To change things before they change *me*.'

He offers me a crisp.

'I'm fine,' I say. 'Change things how?'

Colin looks suddenly very proud indeed.

'I've joined a *class*.'

'A *class*? What *kind* of class?'

'A yoga class.'

'A *yoga* class?' I say, genuinely confused. Colin is not the sort of man you'd readily associate with exercise of this kind. Colin is not the sort of man you'd associate with exercise of *any* kind. 'Why a *yoga* class?'

'I intend to release all my energy blocks!' he says, pointing his finger in the air to make himself look important. 'It will make me supple and toned. And *lithe*. It will make me *lithe* once more!'

'But you always said classes were for girls!'

'Well, they're for *men*, now, as well. *Lots* of men do it. In fact, my class is almost *exclusively* men.'

'They do *men-only* yoga?'

'It is a Gay Men's Yoga Class.'

'But ... but you're not *gay*.'

'I know this. But it's the closest one to my house and also, I bet gay men are a lot less judgemental about the male physique than girls.'

I am struggling to imagine Colin getting into the Lotus position. But he is serious. He is deadly serious. He intends to become a Yogi.

'Is there ... a *name* for Gay Men's Yoga?'

'I don't know. Probably Goga. I'll find out when I start. We have to begin to look after ourselves, Dan. We're in our *thirties* now. We are very old men indeed.'

He looks at me, solemnly, and with what seems to be real pity in his eyes. Is it because he sees in me the man he used to be? The man before self-reflection and Gay Men's Yoga? Is it because I am unenlightened? Is it because ... he has *changed*?

'Shall we have another quick pint?' he says. 'And then I'd better go, because it's curry night.'

No. It is not because he has changed.

But as I trudge home from the pub, I think about Colin's decision. And then I think about why I'm *trudging*. When did I start *trudging*? What has happened to my youthful bounce? Where is the spring in my step? Why do I not feel supple, or lithe? *Colin's* going to feel supple and lithe – shouldn't *I*?

But no, I tell myself. I am just feeling a little worn down. I've been on a book tour recently, eating bad food, stopping at motorway services halfway home from Norwich or Milton Keynes or Birmingham at nearly midnight, buying sausage rolls or cans of cut-price Lilt. This is just a phase, I tell myself. I'll be back to normal soon.

And then I realise that being back to normal still involves sausage rolls and cans of cut-price Lilt.

When I get home, I sit down at my computer.

I type 'supple' and 'lithe' into Google. Something deeply unsuitable comes up. I blink a couple of times but the images stay in there. I think I have seen what Goga can lead to.

I wander into the kitchen and make myself a cup of tea. I'm OK, I think to myself. I may not be supple. But I'm supple-*ish*. I'm lithe-*esque*. That's OK, isn't it?

I notice a crumb on the kitchen floor, and without thinking, I bend down to pick it up. It is *easy*. Ha. Take *that*, Colin.

But on the way up, something *terrifying* happens. As I straighten, I hear myself making a noise. A *strange* and yet strangely *familiar* noise. A sound I have heard my *dad* make. A kind of soft, involuntary 'aah' sound. A sound that signifies the end of a short burst of unusual exertion. The sound he would make after picking up a pencil, or stacking a garden chair.

A *middle-aged* sound.

I run to my computer, and I find a website.

Yoga for Beginners.

There's a telephone number. For a centre a hundred metres from my house. I try and find an excuse – *any* excuse – not to dial. But I can't. Because I want to feel *lithe*. And *supple*. Just like *Colin*!

I pause.

And then I pick up the phone.

TREAT

M y wife returns home from work very tired and a little harassed. I realise this would be a good moment for me to make some kind of effort, like cooking for her, except not cooking, because it should be something that she'd *enjoy*.

'Come on!' I say, grabbing her hand. 'Let's get in the car!'

'Why?' she says, confused. Perhaps she thinks I am going to take her to a fancy restaurant, or whisk her away to a boutique hotel for the weekend. I realise I have to manage her expectations.

'We're going to *Borders*!' I say, delighted. She makes a face which people who do not know her very well would mistake for disappointment. But there is more.

'We're going to buy you that *Sex and the City* DVD!' I say, magnanimously. 'And *then* ... we're going to *watch* it!'

She smiles, and stifles a small yawn, and I feel like a good husband.

Twenty minutes later I am unwrapping the cellophane and slipping the DVD into the player. My wife arranges the wine, and I take a quick look at the back cover.

'A classic!' says Edith Bowman.

Undeterred, I press on.

'For too long,' reads the blurb, 'Carrie Bradshaw has been looking for love in all the wrong places ... but in all the *right* shoes!'

Well, at least that's *some*thing, I think. And then I spot the running time. And I blink. But it remains the same. Two and a half hours. Two and a half *hours*. I flip the cover round in disbelief. Four women walk towards the camera, smiling and carrying bags. As far as I can tell, I am going to be spending two and a half hours watching four women walking towards camera, *smiling and carrying bags.*

But then I snap out of it. This is not about me. This is about my poor, tired wife. I can *do* this. After all, just last week she sat through *Jumper* with me, but at least *Jumper* was an *important* film, about a genetic anomaly that allows a young man to teleport himself anywhere in the world, all the while playing a major part in an epic war that has been raging for thousands of years between fellow Jumpers and those who have sworn to kill them. She is lucky I am so cultured.

We settle on to the sofa and I pour myself a huge glass of wine. The film begins, and she yawns again, and gets comfortable.

An hour later, I realise the film has only been on for five minutes. I am so bored. Not because I am a boy and therefore stereotypically predisposed to another genre of film altogether, but because where is the character development of, say, *Jumper?* In *Jumper*, there were also explosions, and a bit where he ends up on a pyramid. So far, not one of these events has happened in *Sex and the City.*

But I must remain quiet. Tonight is not the night for remarks of this ilk.

I pour myself another huge glass of wine, and silently seethe, as one of the characters makes a sassy remark to one of the other characters about being single or something. My wife seems to be quietly enjoying the film. I swig my wine and think about how many points this must be scoring me, and marvel at the sacrifice I am making. I suppose I am a little like Jesus in this respect, and especially tonight, because tonight *The World's Most Amazing Videos* is on Bravo. Maybe I could suggest a little break in order to watch *The World's Most Amazing Videos*, I think. But no. That is not what Jesus would do. Jesus would watch *Sex and the City* with my wife.

I take another gulp of wine and try and concentrate on what's happening. I have no idea what's going on, and worse, there seems to be no resolution in sight. I am just watching a series of events, one after the other, involving women talking to each other about various things. At least in *Jumper*, there were gentlemen *and* ladies, *plus* they could teleport. I look over at my wife. Her eyelids seem heavy. She clearly feels the same way I do. But it is not my place to suggest watching *Jumper* again. I will wait for *her* to do this.

And then Carrie hits a man with some flowers, and I am shocked into paying more attention, because this is the most action I've seen so far. The flowers explode into the air, and there is shouting, and confusion …

My wife wakes up as the film is coming to an end, what seems like mere moments later. I am staring at the screen and have a newfound respect for Edith Bowman.

'How long have I been asleep?' she asks, and then, 'What's happened to all the wine? Have you been *crying*?'

I make a disgusted face and swig the last of a second bottle.

'No, I have not been doing that!' I slur. 'And if I *had* they would've been tears of *boredom*! Not tears of *joy* and an aching *pain*!'

I look away, and pretend to be studying my phone, but realise it is a remote control and there is not much on it to study.

My wife looks confused and goes to bed.

I open another bottle and stay up and watch the extras.

YOGA

The mere fact that I have booked myself into a Yoga for Beginners course for the following week is enough to make me feel like I am making an effort.

An effort to look after myself. An effort which is mature, and grown up, and metrosexual, and *manly*.

Yes! I think, as I bound down the street. Look at me! I am a *new* man! I am a new man who is *unafraid* of yoga!

It was all Colin's fault, dropping words like 'supple' and 'lithe' into casual conversation. Words he claimed to want to be able to use about himself. Words I hadn't been able to use about *my*self since I was fourteen and as slinky as a slinky.

Not that I ever walked around as a fourteen-year-old describing myself as supple and lithe or as slinky as a slinky. That would have been an odd thing for a child to do, and nothing more than an invitation to bullies. To be honest, I'd have bullied *myself* if I'd done that, and then hand-delivered the invitations to bullies up and down the land straight after.

But now, as a thirty-one-year-old man who finally realises he is in the prime of life and that one day he *won't* be, I am willing to take the reins. To be the change I want to see in the world! To sit on a mat and bend my legs and breathe deeply and emerge supple and lithe and as slinky as a slinky.

But not until next Wednesday, because the teacher's on holiday in Corfu at the moment.

This, though, gives me *time*. Time to mentally prepare myself.

I ring Colin and tell him to meet me at the pub.

'What else can we do?' I ask him, excited, as he sits down. I am drinking a shandy. A *shandy*! This is all part of the New Me.

'What else what?' he says.

'What else can we do that will make us lithe and supple? You know … like things that *ladies* do. Pilates. Or that one where you put hot rocks on your face.'

'How will that help us be supple and lithe?'

'I don't know! But it *must* help. That's why they do it! That's why ladies are all so supple and lithe!'

'I'm not sure I want to put hot rocks on my face.'

'Forget the rocks. We can do other things. We can do *holistic* things. We could chant, or eat incense! We could get personal trainers who'll turn up at our house and make us run around parks! We could get *matching* ones!'

'I suppose I wouldn't mind buying a nice moisturiser,' says Colin, considering my proposal. 'Or some new Lynx.'

I am encouraged. But concerned, too. It had been Colin who had raised our lack of suppleness as an issue.

'We have to think *bigger*, Colin! Lynx won't make us supple!'

Colin takes a deep breath and looks me in the eye.

'This is all because you've booked yourself into a one-hour Yoga for Beginners course, isn't it?'

'Yes!' I say, delighted. 'I am being the change I want to see in the world! Just like you!'

He looks embarrassed.

'Thing is, I'm not actually doing yoga.'

I balk. I am not sure I have ever balked before, or even what it's supposed to look like, but that was a *definite* balk. Colin shakes his head and takes a sip of his pint.

'I never actually went in the end. I decided my time was better spent elsewhere.'

'Where?'

'Here.'

I was annoyed with Colin. How dare he propose we become lithe and then actively de-lithe himself? But then he got me another shandy and I didn't mind so much.

'Well, *I'm* going to continue,' I said, deciding. 'I'm going to see this Yoga for Beginners thing through, and *then* I'm going to see what *else* the world of the metrosexual has to offer.'

And as I say the words, I know I will. This is just the beginning of a whole new me. A me that will embrace the chances afforded me by living in an area of town that has metrosexual written all over it. Not literally, obviously, as graffiti artists find that quite hard to spell.

But an area full of *opportunities*. Full of Ashtanga Centres! Maybe I'll become a Buddhist! Maybe I'll buy some seashells to put in a bowl in my bathroom! Maybe I'll get one of those tiny Japanese Zen gardens and spend idle hours with a miniature rake and some sand! Or a birthing pool! I could always buy a birthing pool!

I will try these things. First I will try Yoga for Beginners – and then I will *change*.

'Enjoying your shandy?' says Colin.

'Not really,' I say.

'Pint?'

'Go on, then.'

SIGNS

A friend-of-a-friend is giving me a lift all the way to Edinburgh in his car.

We have not spoken since we passed Nottingham, but suddenly, the silence is broken.

'Wholesale prices!' he says, completely out of the blue.

'Sorry?' I say. I had been thinking about rainbows, and I'm slightly startled.

'That sign there,' he says. 'It said "Wholesale Prices".'

'Oh,' I say. 'Did it?'

I wait for him to continue, but he doesn't. That was his whole story. He had seen a sign which read 'Wholesale Prices'.

That's strange, I think, turning back to stare at the road. Why would he say that? Why would he see a sign saying 'Wholesale Prices' and think, I'm going to read that out loud to my fellow passenger?

I try and come up with something to say. I scour my mind for stories about wholesale prices, but I've got nothing. I decide to forget about it.

'Pick Your Own!' he says, suddenly.

'Eh?'

'A sign back there. "Pick Your Own", it said. Probably strawberries.'

I nod at him, my mouth slightly agape. I've got nothing about picking your own, either. Why have I got nothing about wholesale prices or picking your own? Surely *everybody* has stories about those two things? We drive on.

'Or raspberries,' he says, sticking his bottom lip out a bit. 'Could be *raspberries*.'

Oh, God, it's me, I think. I am being a bad passenger. I must be. Why else is this man resorting to simply reading out signs that he sees? I've got to come up with something to get the conversation going. I am the passenger. The non-driver. It is my responsibility.

I have a brainwave.

'Have you seen those new space vegetables?' I say. 'It's been in the news. Chinese scientists sent a load of seeds up into space and when they came back down they'd been genetically mutated so that they're now *super*-seeds. A man grew a melon that was eight feet long! Imagine if they did that to *raspberries*! You could sit inside one and eat your way out! You could use it as a sleeping bag or as a giant red igloo! And then have it for breakfast! It's biodegradable *and* nutritious!'

I am proud of my conversational gambit. It was relevant, topical, and posed an important and necessary question – imagine eating your way out of a raspberry! Also, it touched upon issues of global warming, healthy eating *and* new advances in camping technology. I am not a bad passenger any more. I am an interesting and *wise* one.

The man casts me a sideways glance.

'You can already *get* big melons,' he says.

I sink back into my seat. I have to rethink my strategy. I am boring this man to death.

'Pat's Burgers,' he says, as we pass a filthy van in a layby. 'Cup of tea, 50p.'

I try and look interested, but there is nothing interesting about this whatsoever. Why is he just reading out signs?

'I like tea,' I try.

The man just nods, and whistles a bit.

Maybe it's not me, I think. Maybe it's *him*. Maybe *he's* the boring one. Who just reads out signs they see? A *boring* person, that's who. I came up with the perfectly good topic of eating your way out of a raspberry and it was *rebuffed*. Rebuffed in favour of saying 'Pat's Burgers' and telling me how much tea was in a place I'd never see again.

He makes a clicking sound with his mouth. I know what he's doing, and I am filled with dread. He's looking out for something else to read. But there's nothing. And then, up ahead, we spot it. A small brown sign, some way away.

Oh no, I think. He's going to read it. He's going to read the sign. Please, no.

But perhaps I can stop this. Perhaps I can deflect it. Perhaps if I can come up with the perfect topic of conversation, I can halt the inevitable ...

'Do *you* like tea?' I ask, and he says 'yes' but keeps his eyes firmly in front of him.

'What kind of tea do you like?' I ask.

'*Normal* tea,' he says.

'There are all sorts of different teas,' I say, but he doesn't respond. The sign is almost upon us. It can *nearly* be read. It's something to do with *eggs*.

I need to think *quick*!

'I once punched a *kitten*!' I say, a little too loudly.

There is a beat.

The man looks at me.

We pass the sign.

'Not really,' I say, smiling.

I have triumphed, and inwardly I am as happy as I have ever been.

The man taps at his steering wheel, and then, under his breath ...

'Farm fresh eggs.'

My heart sinks. This is what the journey is going to be like from now on. I cannot win.

Up ahead, I see a sign.

'Edinburgh, 200 miles,' I say, and the man smiles.

ORDERS

I am sitting in the first-class section of a train from Edinburgh to London. I don't normally get first-class tickets, but I'm on my way home from a business thing, and the organisers had pressed them into my hands and told me to enjoy myself. It is peaceful in first class, apart from a grumpy chef who informs me he's only got a chicken sandwich left.

It is just one week since I drove up here, the passenger of a man who insisted on whiling away the hours by reading out every sign he saw. But here, I sit and happily eat my chicken sandwich in an otherwise empty carriage. I feel lucky and posh. But then the grumpy chef wanders in from his section of the train and sits down on the chair behind me. He is making odd, grumpy noises with his mouth, and he gets his phone out.

'Hello …' he says, grumpily. 'OK, here we go … Fifteen Pepsi Cola.'

He clears his throat, loudly, and I put my book down and stare straight in front of me.

'Fifteen, yes,' he says and then makes a 'tsk' noise. Perhaps the person on the other end of the phone deems fifteen Pepsi Cola excessive. He carries on regardless. 'Six lemonade, six red wine, eight white wine …'

He stops. He's finished.

He carries on.

'Four Yorkies … twelve gin … six whiskies …'

I turn slightly, to look at him. He is engrossed in his order. It looks to be quite a big one. I am doomed to listen to a grumpy man reading out quantities of random things for two hours. This is not fair. I nearly cried when that other bloke read out his nineteenth sign.

'Three chicken sandwiches ... sliced lemon ... six vodkas ...'

I try to ignore him. I try to go back to my book.

'A hundred plastic cups ... yeah, a hundred ... plastic ... cups ...'

I restart the sentence I'd been reading.

'*Plastic* ones. Yeah. *A hundred* of them.'

I sigh loudly, and restart it once more. I must have patience.

'Two anti-bacterial cups. *ANTI-BACTERIAL*. Thank you.'

We find a tunnel. There is silence. Darkness. Peace. It is short-lived.

'Six lagers. Six bitters. One box of gloves.'

I realise I am not going to get any reading done. I put my book down again and shut my eyes, tight. I am suddenly very annoyed with this man.

'Eight ginger ale. Eight coke. Brrrread.'

Why did he say 'bread' in that annoying way? Who says 'bread' like that?

'Pretzels. Pretzels. *Pretzels.*'

He did *not* need to say that three times. Someone should shove a pretzel in his face next time he does that. *That'd* teach him.

Suddenly my seat rocks back and forth wildly. He is using it to steady himself as he stands, list in hand, and he continues to read. I look around the carriage. Why is he doing this here? Why is he doing this next to *me*? Surely he could have done this literally *anywhere* else? Or in his kitchen! Why do these orders need to be made six inches from my head?

I scowl at him as he wanders up and down my section of the carriage, but he does not see me, until I notice his eyes flicker my way, and I instinctively hide my scowl and change it for a look of polite indifference.

Why did I do that? I think to myself, silently fuming. Why do I look polite and indifferent? I scowled because I wanted him to *see* me scowl! I wanted him to *understand*! He is invading my personal, paid-for space with his loud and pointless list of nonsense!'

He turns his back on me and continues with the order.

I should say something, I think. I should not *fear* my scowl, but *embrace* it. Build on it. *Use* it. This man is in the wrong. He must be *told*! How else will he learn? I must vanquish my Britishness and replace it with something more forthright and European! I will not simply forgive him. I will sternly instruct him to be quiet, or to go somewhere else, and he will do so, shame-faced, and doffing his cap. What am I *afraid* of?

He turns and sees me staring at him, lost in furious thought, but I don't have my scowl ready, so I just look a bit odd. He turns away again.

'Five hot chocolate ... Box of ...'

Look at him. Look at how *rude* he's being. All he had to do was ask me if I minded. Or shoot me an apologetic glance. But no. Oh no, Mr Grumpy Chef has his important Yorkies to order. I feel like pushing him into a big box of anti-bacterial wipes. And then pouring fifteen tiny cans of Pepsi all over him. Look at his stupid jacket and his silly face. I'm going to get him. When we get off the train, I'm going to *get* him. I'm going to wipe the rest of this sandwich all over his hair and then shout 'Brrrrread!' at him for ten minutes. *That'd* show him. I'm a *customer*! This is an *outrage*!

'And that completes the order for the service,' he says. 'Thank you!'

He hangs up, and then puts his phone in his pocket.

Maybe I could trip him up as he walks past and then sit on his shoulders and press pretzels into his ears.

His eyes scan the list, and he taps his lip with his pen as he makes sure he hasn't forgotten anything. He probably has, the big idiot. Satisfied, he puts it away, and starts to walk back towards my table. This is it. This is my moment. My moment to show him just how angry he's made me. To shame him into becoming a better Briton. I get my scowl ready.

'Sorry about that,' he says. 'I couldn't get a signal out there!'

'That's OK!' I say, smiling brightly.

That was nice of him.

SPIT

I am with a small group of strangers at an industry party and I can only hope that none of them has noticed what's just happened. But they have. I can *tell* that they have.

The man in front of me – who I have only just met – was telling a funny story about a car he'd just bought. We had all laughed and rocked our heads back in appreciation. And then *I* had thought of something funny to say.

'If *that's* true,' I said, smiling in anticipation of their excellent reactions, 'surely *someone's* seen it!'

It was a killer line. One woman may as well have slapped her thigh, seeming as she did hugely appreciative of my wise thoughts, which she *should* have been, as I was not charging.

But *I* was not laughing. Because as the words 'surely some-one's seen' had left my mouth, so had something else. I had watched in horror as a small globule of spit had left my mouth and arced quickly and beautifully through the air. It was larger than a normal globule. This was no speck. This was the size of a basketball, if you were the size of an ant.

There were too many S words!, I think, in a panic. *This was not my fault!*

For a second, I think my spitball has simply disappeared into the ether, like a comet entering this man's atmosphere.

It burnt up! I think, with relief. *It burnt up!*

But no. Its graceful, looping arc had continued until it lolloped squarely on to the man's forehead, where it now quietly sat, all pleased with itself.

I dare to wonder if I may have got away with it. But I had seen a nanosecond of horror in the man's eyes. A micro-widening of his eyes and a moment of startled confusion.

He *knows*!

And now, as I squint ever so slightly, I can see it. Right between the man's eyebrows. Can *he* see it? Maybe he didn't see it coming! Maybe he thinks he's just sprouted an instant pimple! Or maybe he saw everything! And *felt* everything! Oh, God – what could that have *felt* like?

He snaps out of whatever he'd snapped into, and starts a new subject. I can tell he wants to get a hankie out and wipe his brow, but he doesn't. He says, 'Sometimes, when you come to these things ...' and I zone out, because I'm concentrating on where my spit has gone. I notice with relief that it's not dribbling. I am not a St Bernard and produce only an average amount of saliva for an adult human male, and so it's far too small to dribble, and what's more, the man has provided *excellent* surface tension. But it's still there. It's *definitely* still there. Just foam and a bubble, probably, but it glistens and twinkles and surely that's enough?

Just act normal, I am thinking. *Even though you have just spat on a man's head.*

The man is avoiding my eye as he talks, waving his hands around, generously forgoing any need to talk about the dark events that have occurred here today. But now, inexplicably, I really want to talk about it. I want to grab his cheeks, and look deep into his eyes, and say, 'I do apologise for spitting on your head,' but I remain silent and secretly try to see whether anyone else has witnessed this horror. The women we are with are all smiling and listening to the man, rapt. Maybe they didn't see. Or maybe they saw and are trying not to look at me in case I start talking and spitting on them as well. I shake my head slightly. I am a spitter. These women think I am a spitter.

But then I wonder ... is this really so bad? After all, did not Jesus spit upon the blind man to heal his eyes? But this man is wearing glasses. Jesus would have purposely *avoided* spitting on him. And also, I am not Jesus.

Maybe I *should* come clean. Say I'm so sorry, highlight the fact, tell him about the tricky sentence, let him know I've made his forehead twinkle. But I can't. I would only embarrass him. And also, there are too many 'S' sounds in saying you're so sorry. I decide it would be best if I simply followed the crowd and pretended the whole thing never happened. After all, we all do it. We have all, at one time or another, inadvertently spat on someone's arm, or face, or on their food. It is a human failing. One we must conquer. And after all, have I not already proved myself a worthy companion with that excellent joke from earlier?

'How about you, Danny?' says the man. 'Have *you* ever been there?'

'Sorry,' I say, briefly and casually covering my mouth, just in case. 'Been where?'

'Cirencester?'

Cirencester. I have the *perfect* joke about Cirencester.

I shake my head.

'No,' I say.

COMEDY

am waiting for Colin to finish work so we can grab a bite to eat in our local.

When he arrives, he is excited.

'There's comedy on tonight,' he says, pointing at a sign. 'I've always wanted to have a go at that!'

This is strange. Colin has literally never once mentioned he's always wanted to have a go at that.

'Why don't you ask them?' I reply, jokingly. 'Maybe they'll let you do five minutes.'

'I will, sir!' he says, and a moment later he's out of his chair.

He sits back down sixty seconds later and I prepare to commiserate.

'They say that's fine,' he says.

'What? What do you mean they say that's fine?'

'They say I can do a quick set between the bigger acts.'

'A quick set? You haven't got a quick set! And what do you mean, "the bigger acts"? Any act in the world is bigger than you! That fella who plays the spoons down the tube station is bigger than you!'

'It'll be fine,' says Colin, waving away my concerns. 'It's just talking …'

But it is not just talking. It is set-ups, and punchlines, and call-backs, and pay-offs, and … you know … jokes. But Colin already has one of those, apparently.

'I've been working on it a while,' he says. 'It'll be good to give it a public airing.'

'You've written a joke? When did you write a joke?'

'During the Beijing Olympics. But it remains topical. It goes like this …'

He casts a nervous glance around, just in case there are any lesser comedians listening in who might be short of a topical joke about the Beijing Olympics.

'So … I'm not racist,' he begins, before adding: 'I love the hundred metres!'

He sits back in his chair, arms out, proud of himself. I remain open-mouthed.

'Are you sure you can make that last five minutes?' I ask.

'Relax, Dan. Everything's going to be fine.'

'But there'll be an audience! What if they don't laugh?'

'I'll riff! And anyway, there's no such thing as a bad audience,' he says, wisely. 'Only bad comedians.'

I can't believe Colin is using words like 'riff' and already counting himself among the 'good' comedians. But twenty minutes later, as he sees his audience of real, actual people starting to make their way downstairs, he realises his mistake.

'What the hell am I doing?' he says. 'I can't make one joke last five minutes!'

'I don't know!' I say, just as panicked. 'Why are you doing this?'

'Quick – give me some jokes!' he says. 'Anything!'

My mind goes blank. I can remember not one funny thing anyone has ever said, ever. But then something occurs to me. I grab a napkin and get a pen from my bag.

'What are you doing?' says Colin.

'It's an Emergency Joke. You can do it if you get into trouble.'

I can sense Colin is rolling the words 'Emergency Joke' around in his head. Psychologically, he now has a crutch. Something to fall back on. He seems brave once more.

'Let's do this!' he says, tucking the EJ into his back pocket, and we walk downstairs.

Inside, the compere has begun, and the crowd is loving it. He banters, he joshes, and the first act enters to huge applause. She is excellent. I can feel Colin bristling next to me, every now and again patting his back pocket for reassurance.

'So, just before the interval,' says the compere, 'let's all have a big hand for a newish comedian who'll be trying out some material tonight ... Colin!'

The crowd claps uncertainly, and suddenly 'newish' Colin is there, on the stage, waving madly at the crowd and shouting 'Hello!' He blinks for a moment as the applause stops, and then says, 'I'm not racist ... I love the hundred metres!'

Somewhere, someone coughs. Others wait patiently for the punchline. Colin mutters something about the Beijing Olympics then looks at his watch. He only has four minutes and fifty seconds to go.

He tries to banter but there are no takers, so he reaches for the EJ and I freeze as he begins to read it out.

'If things are going badly,' he reads, 'simply ask someone in the front row what they do for a living, and when they reply, say something funny about that.'

He picks a man, who says he's unemployed. Colin just stares.

As we walk home in moonlit silence a little later on, Colin stops on a corner and cheers up a little.

'I suppose, on reflection,' he says, 'sometimes it *is* the audience's fault.'

THE HOLIDAY

The sun peeks through the curtains like a nosy neighbour wondering why I'm not up yet. I cover my eyes with my arm, and then my arm with my pillow, but it is no good. I am awake. There is no going back.

I yawn, and groan as I see that the clock says '08.19', but then I remember: I am on *holiday*! Summer holiday! The holiday I've been telling myself I both need and *deserve* for so long now! The holiday that I knew would allow me to leave dank and drizzly London behind and get away from it all – far, *far* away from it all. Far away from the traffic, and the chip shops, and the faceless, everything-the-sameness of modern-day life.

I look over at my wife. She's still asleep, but I want to wake her, and say, 'This is it! We're on holiday! Prepare yourself for culture and fun! Let us throw away the familiar and launch ourselves into a universe of new experiences!' But then I realise that is quite a lot to say to someone at 08.19 in the morning, so I get up and just look out of the window instead.

And there it is. The city, in all its vast, unfamiliar, foreign beauty. Well, *some* of the city. The bits of the city I can see from outside the window of the Marriott.

So this is it, I think, shaking my head, and with wonder in my eyes. The Marriott car park. And there! There in the distance! A Wagamama!

Already, I find myself excitedly planning my day. We could go for a walk through the car park. And then maybe go to Wagamama.

But no. That might be too much too soon. My wife needs to relax. Needs to acclimatise. I have visited this country once before, many years ago. I am *prepared* for it. But *she* will need *time*.

I scribble a note, pull a shirt on, and quietly click the door shut. Before she wakes, I will fetch breakfast. And I will *explore*.

I pad through the sleek, marble foyer of the Marriott like a brave and fearless adventurer of old, pausing only at the entrance to the hotel, where a worn and weather-beaten old man is selling coffees from a Starbucks trolley in the corner.

Who are you, traveller, who stands here today? I can tell he is thinking. What business do you have with my people, with my land?

I do not answer him, mainly because he has not verbalised this, but also because I have started to consider a pastry. I buy my supplies from this wide-eyed merchant, and stride through the automatic doors, like Indiana Jones with a latte.

Outside, the sense of adventure is heightened. The safety net of Western civilisation is further away with every yard I travel. I look back at the Marriott. Fare thee well, old friend, I think. Wish me luck.

I look around me, at the square buildings, with their windows and doors. At the Esso station across the road, full, I am sure, of unusual petrols and diesels. But where am I going? What should I *do*?

And then I spot it.

A Borders.

I stand outside for fifteen minutes, drinking my outlandish latte and waiting for it to open. Familiar-looking cars drive by, but upon closer inspection, *some* of them have *slightly different names*. I shake my head. Ha, I think. They will *never* believe this back home.

Borders opens its doors, like the cave in *Aladdin*, and in I walk, past the latest Nick Hornby novels and the imported copies of that week's *Heat* and *Grazia* magazines. I clamber aboard the escalators, and stride towards the Travel section, with its exotic colours and thick, bound books, where I find a guide to local points of interest and experiences. I hope I will understand this, I think, but it is a *Time Out* guide, and so in all likelihood I will.

I look at my watch. It is just after 9am. My wife will be stirring soon. I should head back, lest she assume I am lost for ever to this strange and mysterious land. I flick through the guidebook quickly. *Excellent*. They have a Hard Rock Cafe here.

I take my goods to the counter, and steel myself for interaction with more locals, but my server's name is Tom and he speaks *excellent* English. I kick myself as I realise I am bereft of local currency, but Tom points at the chip and pin machine and so I reach for my Mastercard. He smiles. I wonder briefly if he has seen a Mastercard before; whether these simple, smiling people will understand how a piece of grey *plastic* can pay for a *Time Out* guide and a copy of *Grazia*. Perhaps, like C3PO in that jungle, Tom will start worshipping me as a god, but no, for he is looking away now, and finishing his McMuffin, so I guess we will never know.

I begin my long walk back down the high street towards the hotel and briefly I fear I am lost. But there, just across the car park ... is that a mirage? No. It is the Marriott.

I slide my room key into the slot in the lift and up we go, right the way up, on and on, all the way up to the third floor.

I creep into my room, just as my wife is waking.

'I've had *quite* an adventure,' I tell her, stroking her head gently.

'That's nice,' she says.

I flick on the telly, and find Sky News. I forgot to get breakfast, so order a full English from room service, and hand my wife that week's *Grazia*.

Outside, it starts to rain, gently. I smile, and shake my head.

Man, it is *so* good to *get away*.

THE WISDOM AND PHILOSOPHIES OF A MODERN MAN: 2

MONDAY

I think a great job to have would be as a door-to-door door salesman, because how do you convince someone who's just answered their door that they need a door? You don't. You just take the day off.

TUESDAY

I think a good way to make the show *Gladiators* more exciting would be to give all the contestants little dogs to run around with while playing their games. It would be a real challenge for the dogs to make it upside-down around the Skytrak, and I bet it'd be funny when all the leashes got caught up in the Gladiators' feet.

Also, all the dogs are rabid, everyone has a gun, and it all takes place in space.

WEDNESDAY

The moment I realised Facebook probably wasn't for me was when this sentence popped up to greet me.

Lee Phillips has removed Young Guns II from his Top Ten Movies.

I stared at it. I read it. I re-read it. I decided I probably didn't need to know it. But now I do know it, and I will know it for ever. Whenever I look at my friend Lee Phillips, I will remember that he used to like *Young Guns II* a lot, but then only liked it quite a lot. Why do I know this? And what happened? Sure, it adds the personal touch to Facebook, but still – I could've used that space in my brain for something about warfare or spelling.

I refuse to be part of this movement that updates people constantly on my moods or thoughts via the internet. If they want it personal, it should be personal. So instead of updating Facebook with random facts, I now phone friends up and shout things down the phone at them before they even say hello. 'DANNY WALLACE HAS JUST EATEN AN EGG!'; 'DANNY WALLACE IS SPEAKING!'; 'DANNY WALLACE HAS A LITTLE BLUE HAT ON!' I then hang up and do not answer when they ring back.

I like to think it adds the personal touch.

THURSDAY

I think a nice way of making us all feel better about the bad things in the world would be if news journalists could make their reports from war-torn regions and drought-stricken plains a little more friendly. A lovely big smile at the end of their piece would cost nothing. And also, why don't they wave?

FRIDAY

My wife was the victim of identity theft this week. A German man had stolen her credit card details and was making various bets through a Frankfurt poker website using her money. This was distressing for her, sure. But how was I supposed to feel? I was now married to a German man with a gambling problem. What's worse is I've tried to get in touch with him, with a view to deciding whether I should move to Germany, or whether he will move here. I am determined to make this marriage work. Should he decide to move over here, I suppose my wife will have to steal someone else's identity before moving on. I have therefore hidden all my credit cards – the last thing I need is those two shacking up. However, if this works out, it will be quite a story for me and Hans to tell the grandkids!

I have asked my wife to settle her poker bills before she moves out.

SATURDAY

Why is it that if a small child runs up to a policeman and kicks him as hard as he can in the bottom, it's considered 'cute', whereas if a grown man – who is perfectly respectable and there with his wife – does the exact same thing, I am both 'in breach of the law' and threatened with a fine?

It's one rule for them and another for us, and it has to stop.

SUNDAY

I am writing this in my local cafe where moments ago I ordered poached eggs on toast. The waiter has just come back and told me that he's talked to the kitchen, but they don't have any poached eggs.

'So no eggs at all?' I said, surprised.

'Yes, we have eggs, but not poached.'

'So ... do you have fried eggs?'

'Yes! Or scrambled.'

'So you have eggs, but ...'

'None of them poached.'

'Well ... could you poach one?'

He thought about it.

'I'll double check.'

Moments later, he reappeared.

'That's fine!' he said, with two thumbs up.

I am getting the hang of Britain.

AUTUMN

POLLARD

Over the past year or so, it has become abundantly clear that I must live very close indeed to Su Pollard.

And not just very close indeed. But *perilously* close. So close that, sometimes, on a quiet afternoon, if you just stop for a moment and listen, you can actually *hear* Su Pollard. It is like I live on the Spotted pages of *Heat* magazine, but am entirely limited to the Su Pollard section.

Wherever I go, I see her. Su Pollard in the newsagents, buying bread and milk. Su Pollard at the pub, talking about Steve Irwin. Su Pollard stopping on the street to talk to dogs, or ruffle children's hair, or put a blue bag in a bin. And what's more, *everyone seems to know* Su Pollard. The man in the butchers. The postman, too, and the odd man with the strange hats who lives in the house on the corner. Sometimes I think it is just me that doesn't know Su Pollard, and it makes me sad, because I reckon me and Su Pollard could be close.

I sometimes consider what the me of the early 1980s would think if the me of now could tell him this. Tell him that one day, I would live in London – the nation's *capital!* – and that my life would be so glamorous and exciting that I would not only *see* Su Pollard, star of *Hi-De-Hi!* and *You Rang, M'Lord?*, but *see her most days*. See her as she chats with dogs or struts about in silver hotpants. I think the me of the 1980s would probably explode, which would be inconvenient at best, as history proves I'd be needed later on in my life.

'Do you think it's strange how I see Su Pollard all the time?' I ask my wife, 'and yet I've never once met her?' We are having dinner in our local pub, and I keep looking around in case Su Pollard walks in.

'I suppose it *is* a bit strange,' my wife replies. 'But what I find *more* strange is how you look at her website all the time.'

It is true. I have started to look at supollard.co.uk. Study it, even. I am unable to explain why. I'll be sitting there, clicking about, and somehow inadvertently end up reading about A Song, A Frock & A Tinkle – the Su Pollard One Woman Show that toured the UK in the 1980s. Or reading up on the very latest in Su Pollard News ('Su Pollard will be appearing on *Loose Women* on July 12th!'). Or finding important Su Facts ('Su came second to a singing Jack Russell on *Opportunity Knocks*!'). It is strange behaviour, and not at all becoming. I begin to realise that I will only be able to stop thinking about Su Pollard if I *meet* her.

'Maybe I should engineer a meeting,' I suggest to my wife, on our way home. 'After all, we've both been on *Loose Women*. We could talk about that for a while and then become great friends.'

'So you'd just knock on her door, and say, "Hi, Su, I've been on *Loose Women*, can I come in and talk about it?" She'd call the police!'

My wife is being silly. She knows Su Pollard would like that. She's seen her, too, just the other night, wearing fishnet stockings and laughing with three gay pensioners.

'You might need to find more in common,' she says.

And then, one day, I am in the newsagents.

It is 9.30, or maybe ten, on a Sunday morning, and I suddenly hear a very familiar voice behind me. It is Su Pollard. She is talking to an old man buying tobacco and she is being even louder than normal. She is telling the old man she's going to be on *The Paul O'Grady Show* soon, which is weird, because he hasn't asked. I freeze. What do I do? I could turn around and smile at her, but she's a bundle of energy and it's intimidating. And then she spots my newspapers. I am carrying the *Observer* and the *News of the World*.

'Oh, you like a bit of rubbish with your papers, do you?' she says, laughing, and I laugh back, a little too loudly. I want to say something back, but she's too confident and raucous and I can't think of anything, so I don't. Su pays for her things and then bowls out of the shop, waving at people.

That was my chance, I think, as I leave. That was my chance and I blew it.

But now, up ahead, I see her. We are walking down the same street, and she is slowing down. What do I do? Do I catch up with Su Pollard? Do I overtake her? Both seem disrespectful somehow. But now she is stooping down. She's spotted something on the ground, between the fallen autumn leaves, and she's trying to pick it up. I can't stop now, I have to keep walking, but it's then that she spots me and she looks embarrassed and I see what it is she's now holding in her hand.

'Er … Find a penny, pick it *up*, and all that day you'll have good *luck*!', she says, showing me the penny; justifying it.

I should smile, and say, 'A penny saved is a penny earned!' or something along *those* lines, but I don't. Something from child-hood kicks in, something from the excited *1980s* me, and I look at her, and I say, 'Give that penny to a *friend*, and then your luck will never *end*!'

And now – unbelievably – I am holding out my hand! It is pure instinct! But it has backfired! I had *meant* to recite a *verse of friendship* – instead, I have *demanded Su Pollard give me her penny*!

She looks at me for a moment.

'I never knew it ended like that,' she says, and she hands it over. She looks annoyed.

But I am happy, because I have met Su Pollard, and she has given me a penny.

THE PHONE CALL

I am in Los Angeles, eating a taco in the sun with my friends Tiffany and Jason.

'So meeting new people in this city's always so hard,' says Tiffany.

'Yeah, new people are *so* hard to find,' says Jason.

But then there's a smile.

Because Jason has a new boyfriend.

'It's no big deal,' he says, lying, before adding, 'It's kind of a big deal.'

'What's he like?' I ask, and Jason picks up his phone and fiddles with it, embarrassed.

'Don't be embarrassed!' says Tiffany, who is eating her taco with a fork, as if she is some kind of Mexican queen. 'Let your *heart* do the talking.'

'He's cool,' says Jason, shrugging, and casting his phone aside. 'Andrew's a great guy.'

He says it in such a way as to suggest he wants to talk about this no more, never again, but what he is *really* saying is, 'Please let's talk about this some more, and instantly.'

'So how *long's* it now?' I ask, which, if Jason were Graham Norton, would result in a reply not fit for print.

'Two months,' he says, which is actually quite a boring answer, and sort of makes me wish he *were* Graham Norton.

'*Two months!*' I say, patronisingly, before adding: 'I think he might be The One!'

I say those last two words in quite an accentuated way, and Tiffany laughs, cheekily, and Jason goes red and joins in, saying, 'Well, maybe he *is*! Maybe he *is* The One!'

'Have you kissed him yet?'

'I have! And it was *wonderful*!'

'Well, then, he's definitely The One. You should *marry* him.'

'I *will* marry him! Two months isn't too soon! We will *marry*, Andrew and I!'

And we all have a little laugh as friends do, and then we smile at each other, and then there is a moment where no one says anything, so we all return to our tacos and hope we're not the first to stop chewing so we actually have to come up with something new to say.

I am momentarily distracted by a fly. It is a pretty fly, as flies go, but not so pretty as I would follow it anywhere. I wonder if anyone has ever followed a fly anywhere. What if there was a fly so pretty that you got up and followed it to Spain? What if a fly …

'Oh, God.'

I stop thinking my important thoughts and look at Jason.

'Oh, *God*!'

Hmm. Jason keeps saying 'Oh, God!' He is holding his phone and saying 'Oh, God!' a lot.

'Oh, God, *what*?' says Tiffany, but Jason isn't listening, because Jason is too busy going white.

'My *phone*,' he says. 'Andrew's is the first number … I must've pressed a button … I've *dialled* him.'

'That's OK!' I say, brightly. 'Say hello!'

'I just left a two-minute voicemail.'

There is a moment where Tiffany and I keep chewing. And then there is another moment, where we slowly *stop* chewing. And then there is another, where we swallow our food, and push our plates away, and look at Jason, who looks at us.

'What have we talked about in the last two minutes?' he says, rubbing the bridge of his nose, even though that's something only people who wear glasses can really do convincingly.

'Well,' I say, locking eyes with Tiffany. 'You said that your new boyfriend was The One and that you had kissed him and it was wonderful and that two months wasn't too soon and now you were going to marry him.'

'*Marry* him?'

'You said marry him,' I say, gravely. 'You said two months wasn't too soon and you were going to marry him.'

We all keep quiet for a moment and take in the gravitas of the situation. Jason sounds like a psychopath.

I see that fly again, and it distracts me for another second, and I am grateful for its input.

'Hey, the phone might not have picked it up!' says Tiff, trying to be little Captain Sensible.

'Look where it *is*!' replies Jason. We do. It is literally inches from our mouths.

As we stare, it begins to ring.

It says ANDREW on the screen. It is quite an angry ring. I don't know how he did that.

'So it's not so hard to meet new people here,' says Tiffany.

'You can find new people if you *try* hard enough ...' says Jason.

That pretty fly lands on my taco.

The phone keeps on ringing.

DEAF

I t is a little after midnight and I am standing in the chip shop on the high street trying to decide if I want chips in pitta, or a sausage in batter.

It's getting colder these days, so I *think* I want the sausage in batter, because the batter looks like a lovely sleeping bag for a sausage.

Outside, a group of youths lean against the window, eating their chips. In front of me, a loud man is asking for another wooden fork, as he 'lost' the last one. The man behind the counter grumpily walks to the stockroom. The first man turns and sees me.

'Oh, sorry, mate … have you not ordered yet?'

'No,' I say, 'but you were here first.'

'No,' he says, both hands up. 'I *insist*. Please order.'

He is doing his best to enunciate, perhaps because he is a little drunk, but every second word comes out far longer than it should, with huge extended gaps between them. Yes. He is *definitely* a little drunk.

'Um … well, I'm not sure what to have …' I say.

'What drink do you want?' he says.

It's a little odd that he's asking me this, since he doesn't work here, but I suppose he's just taking an interest, and that's nice, in a way. The server returns from the stockroom with more wooden forks, and the first man takes one, but doesn't leave. I make eye contact with the server.

'I'd like a Fanta, please,' I say, but before the server can blink, the drunk man has turned to him and, with a finger in the air, said, 'He'd like *one Fanta*, please.'

He turns back to me and waits, expectantly. There is an awkward pause while I decide.

'Um … I'd like some chips …'

The server nods, but the drunk man – on some kind of mission all of a sudden – isn't taking *any* chances.

'*One* serving?' he asks me.

'Er … yes.'

'He'd like *one serving* of chips.'

'Any sauce?' says the server, barely looking up.

'Do you want *sauce*?' asks the drunk man.

'I … yes, please,' I tell him.

'Yes, please, ketchup, please,' says the drunk man.

I don't really understand what's happening here. Why is he acting as a middleman between me and the server? I can *see* the server. He's right in *front* of me. He can hear *every word* I'm saying. And yet now, for some unknown reason, the server has decided to take his instructions from this drunk man. He is no longer looking at me. He is waiting to hear what the drunk man will order for me next.

'You don't have to do this,' I say, trying to politely regain control of the situation. 'Honestly.'

'It is *not* a problem,' he says, closing his eyes and shaking his head kindly. 'You'd do the same for me.'

I consider it. I actually don't think I would.

'Anything else?' says the server to the drunk man. I now might as well not even be here.

'Is that all?' the drunk man asks me, and then, enunciating slowly and carefully: 'Do you want *an-ee-thing* else?'

He sweeps his arm across the glass display cabinet to indicate the rest of the chip shop's wares. I have lost all confidence in my own ability to order.

'Um … maybe a battered sausage?'

'One battered sausage,' says the drunk man to the server.

I start to worry that this is some kind of scam. That he'll ask me to *pay* for his services. Hey – maybe the server is *in* on it. Maybe they do this with *everyone*. Outside, the youths are still there, still leaning on the window. But then I notice … they're gesticulating at one another. Hang on – that's not *gesticulating*. That's *sign language*.

The server bangs the can of Fanta down on the counter.

'There's your Fanta,' says the drunk man, pointing at it.

'Thank you,' I say, unsurely. I reach for the can and open it. I look at the youths. Now it all makes sense. This man thinks I am deaf. Despite all the evidence to the contrary, he thinks I am *deaf*. He thinks I'm with those lads outside, and that maybe I'm a straggler. I look at him again. What do I say? Do I come clean? Surely that would disillusion him? What if he decided *never* to be nice again? But I can't go around pretending I'm deaf in chip shops! I'm probably breaking some kind of European constitution!

'Chips, battered sausage,' says the server to the drunk man.

'Here are your chips and battered sausage!' he virtually yells at me, with a huge exaggerated point towards the counter.

I nod a thank you to him, which he graciously accepts. I put my money on the counter, I take my chips and sausage, and I quickly scuttle out of the shop. As I walk outside, the lads are shoving their rubbish into a bin and moving away. I walk off in the opposite direction. As I walk, I consider the drunk man's actions, and decide that although they were clumsy, I should have been more grateful. He thought he was doing a good thing. He was being a thoughtful citizen. Community-minded. He should be *applauded*. I should go back and tell him.

And then I hear wild shouts from some distance.

'Hey! Mate! Your friends went *that* way! *Maaate!*'

I decide I haven't heard him, and I quietly eat my sausage.

THE MEETING

The traffic's been a nightmare and the parking non-existent, but I make it to the man's office just in time.

'Hello!' he says. 'Thanks for coming in!'

'Sorry I'm late!' I say.

'You're not late,' he says. 'You're bang on time!'

'Sorry for being *nearly* late,' I say, with a jolly face. 'Not that you'd have known if I hadn't told you! And in any case there's no point apologising for something you *haven't* done, is there?'

'Ha ha ha!' says the man.

'I mean, it's not like I should apologise for not scratching your car on the way in, is it?'

'Did someone scratch my car?'

'No ... I'm just saying that –'

'Do you want a coffee?'

'A coffee would be great!'

'Did you have to come far?'

'Nope, just from North –'

He presses the intercom.

'Sarah, can we get a coffee in here?'

'... London.'

'Yeah,' he says, nodding. 'So thanks for coming in!'

'No problem!' I say. 'It's a pleasure to be here.'

'I just thought it might be good to meet up.'

'Yes!' I say. 'Sounds good.'

'Throw some ideas around. See if anything comes of it. So how are you?'

'I'm well!' I say.

'Your coffee will be here soon. Did you have to come far?'

'No,' I say. 'Just from North London. But the traffic was bad.'

'Oh, God! Don't talk to me about traffic. It can be really bad sometimes. I remember once it was *awful*. Did you want sugar, by the way?'

His finger hovers over the intercom.

'No thanks,' I say.

'So listen, I just thought you and me should meet up. Seems we'd be a natural fit to work together on something. So we should just get together sometime, throw a few ideas about, see what happens.'

I blink a couple of times.

'What, like, have a meeting?'

'Yeah. Meet up, shoot the breeze, toss some ideas about.'

'A meeting … what, in the future, sometime?'

'Yeah, man. Where are you based?'

'Just out in North London.'

'Cool. Well, maybe you could come in here.'

I nod, confused.

'Let me just chase your coffee … Sarah, how's that coffee coming along?'

There's no answer. He shrugs.

'What kind of food do you like?' he says.

'I like all different types.'

'Me too,' he says. 'So should I just get Sarah to send you an e-mail with some potential dates?'

'What, for meeting up?'

'Yeah. Just casual, just see what happens, no pressure.'

'So what we're saying is, we should have a meeting?'

'Just a thought. Casual meet up. Compare notes. See if there's anything there.'

'So *this* meeting ...'

'Well, *this* meeting is a kind of informal meeting. The *next* one ...'

'... will be more casual?'

'Exactly.'

'OK ...'

He stands up and extends his hand.

'Thanks for coming in, Danny,' he says.

'No, no, I ... enjoyed it.'

'Sorry about that coffee.'

'Don't worry,' I say. 'I'll have one when we meet up.'

'Far to go?'

'North London.'

'Nice to meet you.'

CAR

I have agreed to give Colin a lift to a party in my brand-new car. Although grateful, he is not impressed.

'This car makes you look like a pimp,' he says, trying to find something on the radio. 'Or a drug dealer! A pimp or a drug dealer!'

I am offended.

'It does *not* make me look like a pimp or a drug dealer,' I say. 'It makes me look like a grown-up. Like a man of responsibility and authority.'

Colin shakes his head, but then considers my comments.

'I suppose pimps have responsibility, in some ways,' says Colin. 'And drug dealers possess authority through their menace.'

I grip the steering wheel a little tighter.

'Plus,' he says, 'you've got pimp wheels. Slightly too large for the car.'

He finds KISS FM and starts to pretend he is a rapper.

'Stop making rapper motions,' I say. 'You look ridiculous. This is a grown-up car.'

I flick the radio back to Magic as Colin spots the turning he needs and says, 'It's just down that road there.'

We turn into a dark street somewhere near King's Cross. There is a grubby-looking massage parlour on the corner and various teenagers eating kebabs and kicking beer cans. I drive slowly as Colin tries to find the right building.

'Look at that man over there!' he says, pointing at someone on the corner. 'Look how nervous he is. He probably thinks you're a pimp or a drug dealer. That's why you're driving so slowly.'

'This car,' I say, trying to give the sentence an air of finality, 'makes me look like a grown-up. Those youths may behave a little better knowing I am nearby, and were that man a criminal of some kind, he is now doubtless reconsidering his ways.'

'He is now doubtless considering your pimp wheels,' says Colin.

'*You're* the one going to a party down a street with a massage parlour on the end,' I say, and he gets out.

I have agreed to collect Colin in one hour – long enough for me to run an errand nearby and for him to pick up some money he's owed without it looking like that was the only reason he went to the party.

I turn the car around and make my way back through King's Cross, instantly feeling calm again. A Phil Collins track comes on the radio and I drive towards Holborn, where I'm dropping off a CD for a friend.

Parked up, I climb out of the car and try to walk away without looking at its wheels.

I can't. And I realise, with some horror, that yes, they do look slightly too big for the car. My heart sinks. Maybe I do look like a pimp, driving around London, delivering packages and collecting people who are owed money.

But no. This is ridiculous. Why should pimps have the last word on wheel size? If they were that bothered, they'd drive tractors.

I drop off the CD, and try and shake off the feeling that Colin has ruined my car.

On the way back, I attempt to think of ways to get revenge. I could say his shoes make him look like a baker. Or that he's got a jockey's hairdo. But I can't quite put my finger on the thing that'll rile him most.

As I'm thinking, I somehow miss my turning. I drive back around to look for it again, but to no avail.

Where's that street gone? I pull up and give Colin a call, but it goes straight to answerphone.

Ten minutes later, and I still can't find that street. I know it's round here *somewhere*, but it's *nowhere*. I've lost Colin. And right now, he's probably outside, waiting for me, near youths kicking beer cans and that nervous man, who was probably nervous because *he was a mugger*! Oh God! Colin's going to be *mugged* by a *nervous mugger*! I have to *find* him!

Panicked, I pull up, and roll my window down.

'Excuse me!' I yell to a passer-by, who eyes me so suspiciously that I *want* to shout, 'I am not involved in prostitution!'

The man sidles slowly closer, and he notices my wheels, but all I need from him is a little information and then I can be on my way, so I make myself sound posh and harmless and I say, 'I'm *so* sorry to bother you, but I need to pick my friend up ...'

He relaxes, and I smile, and then I say, 'Is there a massage parlour near here?'

CATCHPHRASE

I realised recently and with horror that I was a man without a catchphrase.

'Surely *every* man needs a catchphrase?' my friend had said, as we ambled past a park. I laugh, at first, before I realise I am laughing on my own.

'Really? What's yours?' I ask.

'Respect is due,' he says.

'Respect is due?' I say. 'Isn't that *Marc's* catchphrase?'

'I taught him it,' he says. 'So it's mine, really.'

'But you *never* say "Respect is due",' I say. 'You say "Peace peace".'

'But I *could* say "Respect is due",' he says. '"Respect is due" is my *other* catchphrase.'

'So you've got *two* catchphrases? I don't think I've even got *one*.'

'Well, you should get one,' he says. 'They're useful. Not only do they help sustain a level of individuality, but they're very handy when there's an awkward moment and you don't know how to fill it. Take Marc, for example. Whenever he's stuck for something to say, he'll say "Respect is due".'

'That's true!' I say. 'He *does*!'

I think back to the time a tramp in Soho had asked Marc for some money and Marc had said he didn't have any. The tramp had just stared at him, until Marc got a quid out and mumbled, 'Respect is due.'

This need for a catchphrase would seem to be a need that only men have. Very rarely do you find a woman with a catchphrase, perhaps because when you *do* find a woman with a catchphrase, it's very rarely one that you'd want to associate with.

Similarly, it seems only to be men who give any thought whatsoever as to what the title of their autobiography should be. My friend has gone so far as to design a trilogy.

'What are they called?' I ask.

'The first one is called *Life in the Fast Lane*.'

'Good title.'

'The second is called *All or Nothing*.'

'OK.'

'And the third, which I plan to pen in my twilight years, is entitled *Call Me Old-Fashioned*.'

'You sound *exciting*!' I say, kicking some leaves. 'What a life!'

'Respect is due,' he says.

My friend spends a lot of time with his parents.

'So what should *my* catchphrase be?' I ask, suddenly concerned I have missed out on an important part of the boy-to-man process.

'I'm not sure you need one, actually,' says my friend.

'You just said *every* man needs a catchphrase. Hey. How about "Wotchoo talkin' 'bout Wallace?" I could say "Wotchoo talkin' 'bout Wallace?" whenever I've just said something a little silly! Or if I was going to introduce a new topic of conversation! "Wotchoo talkin' 'bout Wallace? Well, I'm talking about speedboats!"'

'It's a little too similar to "Wotchoo talkin' 'bout Willis?", which is the catchphrase from the sitcom *Diff'rent Strokes*,' says my friend.

'I know,' I say. 'That's why it's *good*!'

My friend shakes his head.

We walk on in silence, and I spot a man leaning against a lamppost.

'What about "Stand easy"?' I say. 'I could walk into places and say, "Stand easy!" If someone's getting too excitable or angry, I could say, "Hey, you! Stand *easy*!"'

I am proud of myself. 'Stand easy' is a *brilliant* catchphrase. '"Stand easy" is a bit similar to "Easy now",' says my friend.

'So?'

'So that's my *other* catchphrase. I have *three* catchphrases. And also, "Stand easy" is a little military for you.'

'I can be military!' I say, offended. 'Why can't I be military?'

'Well, unlike many men, you've never seen active service,' says my friend. 'Therefore, saying "Stand easy" is almost an insult to those of us who have. Especially when it's just so you can have a catchphrase. It's a little childish, whereas having a catchphrase is quite grown-up.'

My manhood was now in deep and terrifying jeopardy.

'What do you mean, those of us who have? When did you see active service?'

'Worksop, '91.'

'*Worksop*? Since when did anything happen in *Worksop*? And you were about *fourteen* in 1991!'

'I was in the Combined Cadet Force. I had a beret and camo.'

'You had *camo*?'

'*You* can't say "camo". *You* have to say camouflage. *You* have never seen active service.'

'I didn't realise there were so many *rules* to these things.'

I realise I am not ready to have a catchphrase. Plus, I'm not sure if I really *want* one. Having to say it all the time would be distracting, and I can't say I'm certain I'm ready to completely commit to just the one phrase.

'I think I'll leave it,' I say, heavily.

'Respect is due,' says my friend.

VOICEOVER

am in a small windowless room somewhere deep in the heart of London's Soho, and I have been saying the sentence 'Give *your* pizza *pizzazz!*' over and over again for the past ten minutes.

'Danny,' says the director, 'can you now try it a little more casual?'

I nod and give him the thumbs up, and he presses Record again.

'Give *your* pizza *pizzazz!*' I say, quite casually.

The director shakes his head and presses a button so he can speak in my ear again.

'Even *more* casual!' he says. 'You're very casual about adding the sauce to give the pizza pizzazz! Remember that!'

I slide back in my chair and attempt to adopt a casual pose so's he can see I've taken his direction to heart.

'Give ... your pizza ... pizzazz,' I say, purposely avoiding any sort of exclamation mark.

'Good,' he says. 'Good. But I need it sort of casual ... yet ... *urgent.*'

'Sort of slower but quicker?' I say, trying to understand.

'Precisely!' he says. 'Let's try that.'

I clear my throat and think about how to say something slower yet quicker. He checks I'm ready then presses Record.

'Giveyourpizza ... pizzazz!' I say.

'Again, but different!' he shouts.

'Giveyour *pizza* ... *pizzazz!*' I say.

'Keep going!'

'Give your pizza PIZZAZZ! Give your pizzapizzazz! Giiive your pizza a lot of pizzazz please! *Give* –'

'OK, that's not really working,' he says, waving his hand at me with disdain. 'What we need is more of a sense of *drama* … while at the same time lending the sentence a certain … *throwaway* quality.'

'So … loud … but …'

'Yeah,' he says. 'That's it. Loud but … you know …'

'Quiet?'

'You've got it,' he says, nodding.

'OK … and do you still want it casual but –'

'*Urgent*, yes. Thanks, Danny. When you're ready.'

He takes his finger off the button and presses Record. I stare through the glass at him. He's closing his eyes, ready to see what I hit him with next. I take a deep breath.

'Give your pizza pizzazz?' I try, unsurely. He still has his eyes closed. I add some confidence. 'Give *your* pizza *pizzazz*!'

He has still not opened his eyes. Was it quick and slow enough?

'GIVE your PIZZA PIZZAZZ!' I say. 'GIVE YOUR pizza pizzazz.'

Still no response.

'GIVE YOUR PIZZA PIZZAZZ!' I try. 'GIVE YOUR PIZZA PIZZAZZ!'

Now I am just a man shouting 'give your pizza pizzazz' on my own in a booth. I decide to mix it up a little. Maybe he wants me to ad-lib. Directors *love* that kind of thing.

'PIZZAZZ YOUR PIZZA!' I shout. 'PIZZAZZ IT RIGHT UP! PIZZAZZ IT 'TIL IT POPS!'

His eyes snap open.

'Hmm,' he says. 'I like it, don't get me wrong, I do like it, but…'

'You also don't like it?'

'Yes,' he says.

I am embarrassed, and start to think that maybe he should do it himself.

'Let me put it this way,' he says. 'Imagine you've just come home, and you've got a lovely pizza waiting for you …'

Oh, no. I can see where this is going.

'And you like that pizza, you've been looking forward to it all day …'

But I want to give it a pizzazz.

'But when you come to open that pizza up …'

I realise it needs pizzazz.

'… you see that while it's a *great* pizza, there's something *missing* …'

Pizzazz?

'And you think, What can I do here?'

Pizzazz it.

'And then you realise … you need to give that pizza pizzazz.'

I pretend this has helped.

'I see!' I say. 'Yes. Got you.'

'And that's when you get the sauce out, and you put it on the pizza.'

'Right.'

'Because that's what gives it the pizzazz. Do you see?'

'I do.'

He gives me two thumbs up, and he presses Record.

'Give *your* pizza *pizzazz*!' I say, just as I'd said it the very first time that afternoon.

'Brilliant, Danny,' he says. 'I think we've got it!'

We record it another fifty times.

When I get home that night, I have a pizza. I purposely avoid giving it any pizzazz whatsoever.

One month later, I see the advert on TV. I watch, with bated breath.

'Give YOUR pizza PIZZAZZ!' it says.

It is the director's voice.

THE NAME

am trying to remember the name of the bearded dwarf from the 1989 Sega Mega Drive classic Golden Axe as I wander down the high street with Colin.

'I remember the *baddie*,' I say, as we pass AbraKebabra. 'He was called Death Adder. He'd captured the king and his daughter, and was keeping them prisoner in his sinister jail, somewhere outside of Turtle Village. It was ...'

'Didn't ask you what the *baddie* was called,' says Colin, who is being an idiot. 'Asked you what the bearded *dwarf* was called.'

'I remember that at one point you're on the back of this giant turtle and he takes you across the sea, and then you get to Death Adder's castle on the back of a giant eagle, who ...'

'Didn't ask you that, either. What's the little fella called? The little blond fella with the axe?'

I try and think.

'I remember that you could ride around on pink Bizarrians, of which one was known as a Chicken-Leg, but ...'

And then, from somewhere behind me, a new voice ...

'Danny?'

I turn, mid-sentence, and stop in my tracks. It's a familiar face.

'Danny!' he says.

'Hey, hi!' I say, delighted. 'How are you?'

We shake hands and I smile and then I realise ...

I have absolutely no idea what this man's name is.

Uh-oh.

I have absolutely no idea *what this man's name is*.

'What are you up to?' he says, happily, and I go blank.

What *am* I up to? I now can't focus on anything – even the simplest details – because I can't remember this man's name. What *is* this man's name?

'I was just talking about Golden Axe!' I say, and then I realise that's the *wrong* thing to say, because it involves *Colin*, and if it involves Colin, I'll have to *introduce* Colin, and I *can't remember this man's name*!

I start talking very quickly.

'Soheyhowaboutyouwhatareyouupto?'

I make an intensely interested face. A face which says, forget about everyone around us. There is only us in this world.

'Oh, still working at the pub …'

'Yes!' I say. 'The Crown, you are working at the Crown, that's how we know each other!'

This is intended to show him I know exactly who he is and have details at hand to prove it.

But … *Simon?* Is it *Simon?*

'I'm planning on going travelling soon, though,' he says, and then he glances at Colin.

'Ohtravellingthat'llbegoodit'sgoodsometimestotravel …' I say, trying to bring the focus back to me, but I can feel Colin getting impatient, annoyed that he hasn't been introduced yet, but I can't stop. 'And what are your future plans?'

'Well … there's the travel, like I say,' he says, slowly.

'Yes, apart from the travel, though, what are your future plans?'

'Erm …' he says, looking to the skies, and while he does so I steal a quick glance at Colin, who frowns at me, but I can't shrug or give him a help-me with my eyes because now the man in front of me is looking at me again.

Darren!

No!

Paul?

'I guess just chilling out for a while,' says Simon/Darren/Paul.

'That'sgood,' I say, nodding vigorously. 'Goodplangoodplan.'

I pause for a second because I don't know what else to say, and there is that awful nothingness where it becomes incredibly apparent that something must be wrong, and to fill it, for no apparent reason, I laugh like a little lady.

'Aha ha ha!' I laugh, lightly, as if I might be wearing a bonnet and carrying a parasol. 'Aha ha!'

Colin breaks the silence with a manful extension of his hand.

'Hey, man,' he says. 'I'm Colin.'

'Matt,' says the man. Who I suppose I should start calling Matt.

'Nice to meet you,' they both say.

'Sorry!' I offer, making a great show of it. 'I thought you guys *knew* each other!'

This would be a great excuse. If I didn't know Matt from a pub in Bristol.

Matt just shakes his head and says 'no', gently, and Colin simply smiles at me, broadly. I've been caught out. Matt knows I forgot his name. There is nothing more shameful, more nightmarish, more insulting than this.

As we walk away, two awkward minutes later, I am still shaking my head as we pass Currys. I will never recover from this.

And then I suddenly remember something. 'Gilius Thunderhead!' I shout.

'Too little, too late,' says Colin.

HAIR

I t is awful being caught, when you know you've been doing wrong.

But there is something liberating about it too. At last, the guilt has a reason to be there – the guilt that has lain heavy on your shoulders for so many months of secrets, and lies, and deception. Months of dashing around, of avoiding certain streets. Months of illicit meetings in Soho and nervous glances on street corners.

What if they see me? I'd think. What if someone they know sees me?

But you keep going, because that's the situation you're in now, and you either deal with it, or you stop. But you can't stop. Because you've started now, and you're in it up to your neck, and besides … it feels so right.

The man who used to cut my hair is called Tom, and he was a good man. He was solid. Dependable. Honest. He didn't deserve what I did to him, but I couldn't help myself. Our relationship had started several years before, and when he'd opened his own hairdressers in fashionable Soho, I'd followed him there. In the early days, it had been exciting. He'd try new things, make jokes, tell me little facts about himself. And he listened to what I had to say – really listened. But soon, something changed. He'd suddenly be away on courses, or on holiday, without having told me. Our meetings became predictable. He'd give me the same haircut every time, because he knew what I liked. There was no spontaneity. The sparkle had gone. He'd become distant.

We always said we'd go for a pint one day, but it never happened, and soon it felt like it never would.

We were just two people going through the same old routine. And then I met Joe.

It was a big night for me – I was hosting the Constructing Excellence Awards 2008 – and I had to look my best because, boy, the construction industry knows a good haircut when it sees it. I put a call in to Tom to see if he could fit me in. But he was away. On a course.

It's all about the job with him, I thought. His career always takes priority.

I'd resigned myself to celebrating the best of the construction industry's practices and practitioners with an unkempt head of hair. And then I thought, no, the construction industry deserves better, and I walked into a rival hairdressers, which is where I met Joe.

Joe cut my hair brilliantly. Maybe it was the guilt. Maybe it was the unfamiliarity. But it was exciting.

That night, I wowed the construction industry. I talked passionately about the unique bridge between industry, clients, government and the research community that Constructing Excellence provides. I made a joke about architects. I high-fived a CEO, and congratulated him on his work in attracting new clients, cementing existing contracts and building strong links between regional merchants and suppliers.

In short, I had the new confidence a fresh relationship brings.

A few days later, I got a call from Tom.

'Hey, I heard you tried to get an appointment. Sorry about that. Do you want to come in this week?'

'Um, sure,' I said, but then I realised I couldn't. My hair was cut. Cut, by another man. He'd realise. 'But I'm a bit … busy this week. Maybe next week. But soon.'

'Oh,' said Tom.

Did he know? Had I been that obvious?

I carried on seeing Joe. Eventually, Tom stopped calling. Joe suggested I grow my hair a bit longer – something Tom had never seemed interested in – and we agreed to go on this magical journey together. Just me and Joe, and my various hairs.

But this week, as I was leaving Joe's salon, laughing, I stepped into the cold winter air, and on the other side of the street, I saw him. Tom. Just standing there, staring at me. He looked sad.

I didn't want him to find out this way.

'I just … You weren't around, and …' But nothing I could think of to say seemed right. Maybe Tom and I could still be friends, but it seemed doubtful now. Most of what we had in common was physical, and here I was, with fresh evidence, my hair just cut, and by the hands of another man.

'It was the night of the Constructing Excellence Awards,' I wanted to say, by way of explanation. 'A night where it seemed *anything* could happen.'

But Tom deserved better than that.

'Come on,' I said. 'Let's have that pint.'

THE FLIGHT

We look at our tickets and still can't quite believe it.

'They got us first class!' I say, shaking my head. 'There'll be proper cutlery! Fine booze! I think at night the stewardesses cradle you in their arms and stroke you to sleep! You go out for cocktails with the captain afterwards! This is going to be *great*!'

'True,' says my wife. 'But we should play it cool. We must *not* look like competition winners.'

We both put on our bored faces and walk towards the self-check-in machines. I lay my passport on the scanner and make a big show of what a hassle international first-class travel is. I roll my eyes at my wife and I see her smile. We don't belong in first class. Which is why it's such fun.

But then I look at the screen. 'Passport Not Recognised.'

I scan it again and break into a small sweat. The same thing happens.

'Well, that's that, then, isn't it?' I say. 'There's no way we're flying today. Typical. We'll probably have to walk.'

'Or we could just check in normally,' says my wife.

Yes. We could just check in normally.

We wander over to a huge queue and a lady asks to see our ticket. I smile, knowingly. Any second now, she will see the words 'First Class' and point us to a special desk. She will probably summon a fine steed to take us there. Or maybe she'll get us a limo!

But she doesn't. She just smiles and says, 'That's fine.'

Eh? What about the special check-in?

'Um … is there a first-class check-in?' I say, quietly.

'I'm sorry?'

'A first-class check-in? We've got, um, first-class tickets?'

'Sorry, you've got …'

She looks me up and down for a moment, which is a cliché, but I can't apologise for it, because it is *her* cliché, not mine, and if she's worried about being seen as clichéd, she should really re-evaluate her behaviour. She looks once more at the ticket and says, 'Oh. OK. Just over there.'

We thank her and walk off. But something is niggling me.

'She didn't say "sir",' I say. 'She should've said "sir"!'

'Yes,' says my wife. 'You could be anyone. You could be an internet millionaire!'

'Yes!' I say. 'Or a rock star. Or a film director. Or …'

Hang on. An internet millionaire?

'Why an internet millionaire?' I say.

'Just … you know. You *could* be. *She* didn't know.'

'Yes, but why an *internet* millionaire? Why not just a *millionaire*?'

'I don't …'

'Why specifically the internet? Why is that the first thing that pops into your head? Couldn't I have made my money in something else? Perhaps I am a famous property developer. Why do you not think I am a famous property developer?'

'I'm just saying …'

'It's because I wear glasses, isn't it?' I say, highly offended.

'No!' says my wife, and from her reaction I know that it definitely is.

'You think I look like I work on the internet!' I say, in disbelief. 'Out of all the jobs in the world, that's what you think I look like I do. An internet millionaire.'

I cannot believe it. I have married a monster.

'Anyway, I said "billionaire",' she says. 'I said "internet *billionaire*".'

'It's not the money!' I say. 'Probably some of my sites are doing very well indeed, and I'm sure as the economic downturn makes an upturn, yes, we'll see some real profit in the third quarter! But you said *millionaire*, and you also said *internet*!'

'Well, I made a mistake,' she says. 'I meant to say rock star.'

'Yes. Thank you. I am a rock star.'

We turn to face the lady at check-in who's heard the last few seconds of our conversation. And then I remember that I am not a rock star and that someone else has paid for our tickets. We suddenly feel like competition winners.

On board, my wife reads *Cosmo* and sips champagne. I try and find something to watch but the entertainment system isn't on yet and all I can find are CNN Business & Technology reports.

Internet millionaire, I think, shaking my head.

My wife looks at me.

'I said *billionaire*.'

I sip my champagne, grumpily.

TADPOLES

I am back in London, and in the pub with Colin. We have spent the past hour or two exchanging important wisdom and philosophies. But then Colin drops a bombshell.

'It's not just the robots, Dan,' he says, shaking his head and putting his pint down. 'I mean, the robots will obviously have their place in our inevitable destruction – it's *logical* – but we will have our *own* part to play.'

'How?' I say, horrified. 'How will we have our own part to play?'

His eyes dart nervously around the pub. I lean in closer.

'According to reports, Dan, we can no longer rely on our own ... little beasts.'

I try and work out what he means.

'Cats?' I say.

'No. Our ...' He glances nervously again. '... internal tadpoles.'

'Oh!' I say, realising. 'Why? What've they done?'

'It's what they're not doing. A man's IT count is down ninety-four per cent from sixty years ago.'

'What? How do you know this?'

'A report on the internet. From Mexico.'

That's something you don't argue with.

'It's to do with salt, Dan. And soy. And beer.'

'But I *like* beer! And salt! And we've got a bottle of soy sauce at home!'

'Hmm. Have you ever opened it?'

'Of course not, no. But the other stuff!'

'Well, I'm just saying. Children are no longer a right. It's really got me worrying.'

He takes another huge sip of beer.

'How many tadpoles are you supposed to have?' I ask him. He is suddenly the font of all knowledge, and I need him.

'If it's anything under twenty million, it's not quite enough.'

Twenty million?! That sounds a *lot*! Never before have I questioned my internal tadpoles. I'd never even really considered them. But now that Colin has questioned them citing this important internet report from Mexico, I suddenly realise – I'm infertile! I *must* be! We *all* are!

'But I won a swimming competition when I was nine!' I plead. 'I was North Leicestershire Under Tens Breaststroke champion! Surely that counts for *something*?'

'Swimming quickly is not hereditary,' says Colin, wisely. 'Otherwise we'd have babies in ponds, and all you'd have at the Olympics were thousands of men called Goodhew.'

God, Colin is clever sometimes. Why can't I be more like Colin?

Later, at home, I avoid talking to my wife. I am ashamed. I open the cupboard and check the soy sauce bottle for warning labels. There aren't any.

Suddenly, every advert on TV features a small child, or a hapless father being bullied at the breakfast table by his unpleasant family. For the first time, it pulls at my heartstrings. I can be hapless! And what if one day *I* want an unpleasant family?

Children are something we've talked about, but it's never felt real until now. And what if it's not possible?

I decide to book in for a test. Already I'm nervous. What if I haven't got twenty million? What if I've only got *one*? I was quite a big baby, so maybe I've only got just one really big one? I'm not sure if this is how it works.

I arrive at the hospital.

'What are you here for?' says the lady behind reception, and my stomach flips. I have to tell her. And then she'll *know*. Worse, she'll know what I'm here to *do*. I just hold up the letter confirming the appointment and she looks away quickly and mumbles 'downstairs'.

Downstairs, I take my place on a hard chair in a literally sterile waiting room. I exchange a pained look with another man.

He knows what I'm about to *do*, I think, shaking my head. Moments later, he shakes his head too. This is all Colin's fault! Why couldn't he have just stopped at the robots? Every sip of beer will now feel like *murder*! Colin has ruined my life!

'Mr Wallace?' says a male nurse in a green uniform. He is holding a small container.

I stand up, and steel myself. The other man looks at me. We exchange a nod of solemn solidarity. We are men. Men, together. Bonded by paranoia, and society, and convention, and possibly inaccurate Mexican internet reports.

I take the small container and consider it. Clearly, the nurse holds no great hopes for me. How you're supposed to get twenty million of *anything* in one of these I've no idea. I must prove him wrong. Prove that the Wallace bloodline can and will continue.

I remind myself of that day in Loughborough Leisure Centre – the glorious final lap, the roar of the crowd – and think, I can *do* this.

I walk into a small room.

CHILDREN

We have been shopping in town and are on our way home on the tube, laden down with bags and coffees.

Opposite us sits a small child in a buggy, his mother stroking his hair and doting. I watch my wife melt a little and she smiles at the boy, and waves. He smiles back, and looks to his mother, then back at us.

And then he looks at me and starts laughing inexplicably. My wife laughs, and I laugh, and I pull a funny face and everyone laughs.

We get off at the next stop.

That was a nice moment, I think, as we ride the escalators, and I notice my wife is squeezing my hand, warmly. Clearly, she is thinking what a wonderful father I will make, and all because I have the ability to pull funny faces at children.

As we walk down Upper Street, we stop outside a toyshop and look at the small wooden animals. There's another child in a buggy and this time, with no hesitation, I launch into my funny face routine. She's delighted, and claps her hands together, and her mother looks round, and sees me doing my funny face, and she looks delighted too.

This is amazing! I think. I'm some kind of joy-bringer!

We walk home, my wife clinging tightly to me, and when we get there she brings me a beer and lets me watch *Gladiators*.

There has been some kind of shift in the way children view me. Up until recently, they seemed to look at me with dark suspicion or disdain. Or I was an irrelevance to them, just a big, lolloping shape, shifting about nearby, scuttling around with a copy of *Metro* or an iPod. Nowadays, it seems, I'm some kind of potential *friend*. And all since I discovered the funny face. Does everyone know about the funny face? Why had no one told me about the funny face?

And then, a day or two later, I am sitting on the tube, heading for home, when I look up from my paper and see a small boy in a buggy, staring at me. He looks unsure of me, with big wide eyes and a concerned face. I turn my iPod off and smile at him, but he still just stares at me, as the carriage jolts around.

Poor thing, I think. All this noise. All these strangers.

I look at my paper again, because I'd just been reading a very interesting article about a fisherman whose feet went blue, when I remembered something: the funny face. The smiles and laughter I'd brought to London's children. The joy and warmth and delight in my wife's dancing eyes when she'd realised children now respond to me – that I was *at that age*. That they saw in me not a stranger, but a mentor, a father-figure … a *hero*!

I put the paper down again and look at the boy. He starts to smile almost immediately. I smile back. This will be great. Has he seen the funny face before? I wonder whether to build up to it, or just launch straight in, and I start to remember when I was a kid, and a stranger had shown an interest, and I glance around the carriage and lock eyes with his mother and realise I've been staring at her child for a little too long.

Instinctively, I look away, and continue reading about the fisherman and his blue feet. But then I start to bristle.

This is ridiculous, I think. I was going to do her a favour! I was going to bring joy to that small child! I'm his hero, after all!

I look up, cautiously. The mother has relaxed and is staring at her fingers, trying to get some dirt off her ring. I look at the little lad.

Why *shouldn't* I entertain the little ones of this world? Are they so much less important than us? Are their ideas of any less value? Well, yes, but should that stop me making faces at them on trains? No!

And then I see his mum is staring at me again, hard. And I realise that once again I've been looking at her child for a little too long.

'But I was building up!' I want to shout. 'I was building up to the funny face!'

I can *save* this. I try to smile and raise my eyebrows in a non-threatening way, and then I gesture at the kid, and I say, in as confident a way as I can, 'Nice little boy!'

The words hang in the air. People look up from their papers. I think about what I've just said.

I have been caught staring at a little boy on a train – twice! – and then loudly said three of the most sinister words I could.

I don't know what to do.

I do the funny face, but then realise I'm doing it to the mother and at the last second switch to the boy.

He does not look impressed.

I get out two stops early and walk home, avoiding the toyshop.

THE TEST

So you did it?' asks Colin, amazed. 'You really did it?'

'I did, sir!' I say, importantly. 'I did!'

I had been a man. Faced my fears. Stood up to the paranoia of the age. Been for a sperm test.

Maybe, I think, that's why children have been viewing me differently recently. Maybe it wasn't the funny face. Maybe it was the *test*!

'What was it like?' asks Colin, eyes wide and full of respect.

'I will not speak of these things,' I tell him, calmly, like a gladiator might tell something to an overawed peasant. 'These things are not for gentlemen to discuss.'

'Sorry,' he says, embarrassed.

'You will learn in time.'

He nods his understanding and leans back in his chair.

But then he leans forward again.

'Does a nurse do it, or do you do it yourself?'

'Silence, Colin,' I say. 'You must walk this road on your own one day.'

I look away.

'I will have a packet of peanuts now.'

He stands, immediately, and heads for the bar to fetch me some peanuts. I am clearly the alpha male now. For I have done something extraordinary. Something Colin never thought I would do when he told me about a possibly inaccurate Mexican internet report predicting the end of male fertility.

I cast a look around the pub. I am like a king here. I look at other men, blithely chatting with their friends, or sipping spritzers with their wives, and I wonder whether they too have seen that internet report. I want to reassure them, to let them know that the human race is in safe hands, that I will make *sure* we continue. But that might be quite an odd thing to walk up and tell someone you've never met, so I decide simply to remain where I am, and look wise. I am sure, subconsciously, when they look over and see this noble man, in his Sensible Soccer T-shirt and grubby grey Converse, they *know* it's all going to be OK.

I suppose this is a little like my gift to the humans. There is no need to thank me.

'One question,' asks Colin, sitting back down and offering me peanuts, as a simple tribesman might offer his god a goat. 'Can I ask one question?'

I raise my eyebrows and gesture a yes, magnanimously.

'How do you feel, now?'

I ponder his question as I open the peanuts and slowly select one to eat. I have decided to eat them one by one, as Caesar might have eaten a grape.

'I suppose I feel ... good.'

'No, but ... does it not make you feel nervous?'

'Nervous?'

'Yeah ... like, this is it, now? You know why you're here. Here on earth. Has it not brought it into sharp focus? The fact that we're infinitesimally small, here for a blink of an eye, and our only mission, the one shining light in our otherwise drab and worthless lives, is all about one moment, when moons must be aligned, and chance on our side, when luck and biology and purpose collide?'

His eyes are bright and his voice full of passion but he's yet to finish. He points at me, proudly.

'And now *you*, my friend, sitting there ... *you* have made the first few brave steps towards *achieving* that purpose!'

He is right. I have. And all in a small room near a Ryman's.

'So how did you feel,' he says, 'if you'll permit me one last question, when the results came back?'

I smile. I offer him a peanut, but he knows his place, and politely declines.

'Well,' I say, popping one in my mouth. 'Obviously the results aren't instant ...'

'No,' he says, unsurely. 'But when you got them, how...'

'Well, I haven't technically *got* them,' I say. 'Not *yet*.'

'You haven't *got* them?' says Colin.

'Not *yet*,' I say. 'It takes a couple of weeks.'

'So you don't *know* yet?'

'What's to know?' I say. 'But I did it! And I've got a good feeling!'

Colin just stares at me. He is probably still a little overawed.

'I will have a pint now,' I say, waving him towards the bar.

He grabs the packet of peanuts, and finishes them off in one.

TOMATOES

T he man I've invited round this evening is talking about his recent break-up and becoming very emotional. We're in the kitchen, bonding like men, and I'm stirring the pasta, because the pasta isn't going to stir itself.

'It had all been going so well,' he says, and his eyes glisten, as he shakes his head and looks towards the ceiling. I make the appropriate response, and roll my eyes when he tells me of things she said, and nod and shrug when he tells me the very sensible things he said back.

I reach into the cupboard for a can of chopped tomatoes, and he enters Stage 2: the moment he suspected things *weren't* going so well.

I can't look away at this point, so I feel around the lid while he speaks, but there's no ring-pull, so I keep nodding as I find the cutlery drawer, and open it, and start to blindly grasp about for an opener. This makes a lot of noise, though, so I stop until the small window of opportunity before Stage 3 – the moment he *knew* things weren't going so well after all – and I use it wisely, quickly glancing at the drawer and rooting around until, bingo!, I find it.

I smile to myself, and he says, 'What?', and I realise a smile is not appropriate.

'Women!' I try, shaking my head, and he relaxes, and says, '*Exactly*.' This seems to work in almost any post-break-up situation.

I take the can opener and try to fix it to the lid of the can, but this is easier said than done, especially when Stage 3 requires intense looks of deep understanding and concern. But this man needs pasta! He hasn't eaten in two days! He needs *my* pasta!

He casts a faraway look out the window, and I act fast, attaching the can opener to the can and squeezing the handle down. I'm in!

He looks back at me and I hide my delight once more, but this time I start to wind the opener round, which is good, because I purse my lips when I do it, and it makes me look a little angry.

'But then – get *this* ...' he says, and I stop winding to show I am all ears, but I can feel that the can opener has lost its grip on the can slightly, and I am annoyed. I shake my head and look to the ground, in a can't-believe-she-did-that way, but really, I'm looking at the can and trying to get the opener back on. I manage it, and begin to wind, but immediately it pops out again.

'Dammit,' I say, and once again, my friend says, 'Exactly.' He continues to talk, and I force the opener to bite into a new part of the lid, but the same thing happens again.

Who *invented* this? I think.

'And do you know what *she* said?' says my friend, selfishly interrupting my important thoughts.

'No?' I say, and then try and find another area for the can opener to try.

'She said it was *my* fault!' he says.

'No!' I say, and then I smile, because I'm in again! He laughs and I laugh and then we are two men laughing.

'But ...' he says, and I look down at the can. I've managed to cut into the lid maybe six or seven times around one side. If I can just cut in between them and link all the cuts together, I can *do* this ... so I focus on the can, but keep shaking my head while my friend talks, and I use the opener to make more little cuts until I'm three-quarters of the way round. Almost there! All I now have to do is force the lid down! But I must wait for my opportunity. I look my friend in the eye while he enters Stage 4: why he *should* have known things weren't going so well. But this is a tricky stage, because it's full of regret, and blame, and angst, and I have to wait until the second he's lost in his own thoughts ...

'And that was it, you know?' he says, finally. 'She was *gone* ...'

He looks away, tears in his eyes, and I press down hard on the lid ...

Fffffblat.

This is awkward.

I now have freshly chopped tomatoes up my shirt, up my face, on my glasses, and there is a streak of freshly chopped tomatoes heading up the wall. There is tomato on the ceiling and a piece in my ear.

It seems when you force your hand into a can of freshly chopped tomatoes, the freshly chopped tomatoes are quick to find somewhere else to go.

When he looks back at me, he just blinks. We stare at each other. What do I say? We were on Stage 4! You can't introduce slapstick on Stage 4!

'Women,' I say, again, and there's a pause.

'*Exactly*,' he says.

CAREERS

It is a little after ten o'clock at night, and I am riding a loud and clattering overground tube back to North London.

The carriage is relatively empty. An old lady studies a Sodoku pamphlet on the seat opposite. Two Japanese students are asleep with their feet up, to my left. We are all quiet and anonymous, which is the law.

But just several metres away stand three drunk men, roaring with laughter. The students sleep through it. The old lady concentrates on her Sodoku. The men roar with laughter again. They are talking about the Japanese students and pointing.

'Him, right,' says the first one, thinking he's whispering, 'he's probably, like, a *karate* instructor!'

His friends splutter and high-five each other.

'What about his mate?' bellows his friend. 'Guess *his* job!'

'Him? Probably, like … a shark … fisherman?'

His friends don't find this quite as funny, and instead of laughing, they shrug and sip at their beers. But they want to recapture the brilliance of their pal's first incredible observation, so they persevere.

'What about *him*?' says one.

They are pointing at a man I hadn't even noticed, slumped against the window, a copy of *The Times* on his lap and a little bit of drool inching its way from his mouth.

'Him?' says the first man, now with everything to prove.

'Yeah!' say his mates. They can't bloody *wait* for this.

The first man looks at the sleeping stranger. He has a window of approximately two seconds in which to make his joke, otherwise it will wilt and die.

'That bloke probably works ... at a *drool* factory!'

It is rubbish, but it is quick, and sometimes that's all that matters. His mates go crazy, whooping and stamping the floor, but still thinking they're being very quiet indeed.

The old lady closes her eyes. We both know I am next. I close my eyes and pretend to be asleep.

'What about *that* one?' says one of them.

'That one with the glasses?' whispers the first.

There's a pause as we go through a tunnel. The train screeches and the carriage jolts and the lights flicker slightly. It gives the first man valuable thinking time. I hate this. I *hate* it when people look at you on the tube. It's not *right*. It shouldn't be *allowed*. The whole *point* of sitting on the tube is not to draw attention to yourself. We exit the tunnel.

'I reckon that bloke with the glasses is either ... a *librarian* ...'

His mates start to giggle.

'... or ... a *male escort*!'

They erupt. It's a *home run*.

'A male escort!' says one of them. 'Brilliant!'

'A librarian!' says the other, but I'm not convinced he's on the same level as his mates.

I open my eyes and pretend to wake up. The old lady's eyes remain shut tight with embarrassment. When they see I am awake, the men look away, and sip at their cans, before breaking out into helpless laughter. I don't know how to act. I have no right of comeback. I have not been invited into their joke.

'What about her?' the most drunken of the three virtually shouts. 'What about that old one?'

This time, the second bloke tries his luck. He's not offered a punchline before, but now he's buoyed by the atmosphere and encouraged by his friend's excellence.

'Her? She's probably …' He pauses. '… an *old* … one!'

I am not sure he's really understood the rules to this game. His friends pause, at which point I think they're probably OK, but then they laugh and laugh, and I look at the old lady, and I think, *Just keep your eyes closed, these idiots will be getting off soon, please don't be insulted.* She keeps her eyes shut, and it makes me sad.

And then we're at Finchley Road, and there are people waiting, and the carriage fills up quickly, and the men keep quiet. The old lady still has her eyes shut, and I want to tell her it's OK, that these guys have to keep quiet now, and they do. They keep quiet. Quiet, all the way back to Baker Street.

And as the train screams its way into the station, the old lady finally feels brave enough to open her eyes, and fake-yawn, and she gets her things together, and the doors open.

'Mate,' says one of the men, squeezing through the crowd. 'Can you settle a bet for us?'

'Yup,' I say.

'What do you do for a living?'

His mates are standing behind him, giggling. I take a deep breath and look the old lady in the eye and smile. She smiles back, unsurely. I look at the men again.

'I am a librarian,' I say, and they raise their eyebrows. 'But on weekends, I work as a high-class male escort.'

They screech and high-five, and run from the train, whooping. They have not understood the revenge the old lady and I are sharing.

I look at her. She smiles. We have *won*.

TECHNOLOGY

I am driving in my car when suddenly I hear a noise that's become far too familiar.

Brrrrp. *Brrrrp.*

I look at the dashboard. Oh, no.

For the past several weeks, my technology has turned against me. My kettle broke. My Xbox gave up. For reasons I am yet to fathom, my Sky box now brings me regional programming instead of the advertised ones, and chooses news from the West Midlands. And my car decides to tap into the BlueTooth network in order to constantly and inexplicably call my friend William.

At first, it was fine. I would say, 'Ha ha! I don't know what happened there! My car has phoned you up!'

'Ha ha!' William would reply, delighted. 'How silly!'

And even when it happened twice in the same day, it was somehow charming and bumbling and fine.

But then it did it *again.*

Brrrrp, I heard. Brrrrp. And then, those two heart-stopping words on the dashboard.

Calling William.

'But I don't *want* to call William,' I'd plead, just in case this car that can make calls on my behalf can also hear what I'm saying. 'I've called him far too many times already! I've got nothing to *say* to him!'

But the car would ignore me, and continue to call him, as if to say, '*You* may have no business with William this day, but what about me? I am just a car to you, aren't I?'

'Hello?' William would answer, and I would keep quiet for a moment, hoping he might perhaps hang up, or get distracted and lose his phone.

'It's … me again,' I said. 'My car keeps calling you up.'

I don't know why my car keeps doing this. William's only been in it once, and it's not like they talked or anything. But I must have phoned him once in here. Must have *trained* the car to think I can't go five minutes without speaking to him. It's got an automatic headlights function. Perhaps there's an automatic William function.

There has to be a bug in the BlueTooth software, I think, sagely, and then I realise I don't even really know what that means, and to be honest, I'd better come up with something to say to William when he answers.

Brrrrp.

Hang up!, I think, pressing the button that looks like it should be the right one. But the arrogant car ignores me.

After the first few times it did this, I'd tried to get away with it.

'Hey,' I'd say, confidently. 'Just thought I'd give you a quick call! To, um, say cheers for the other night!'

And William would say, 'Yes!', and then there'd be a pause, where we'd both slowly realised I'd said this the *last* time my car had decided to phone him.

It could be worse, I think, as the brrrrps continue. There are worse people in my phonebook the car could have chosen to pester every time I drive somewhere. A dentist, maybe, or a cab firm. I'd have to keep ordering cabs to drive alongside me, wherever I go!

And then my blood runs cold.

Or Les Dennis! I've got Les Dennis's number! What if my car kept phoning Les Dennis? Maybe it does! Maybe every night when I park it, it calls Les Dennis! Maybe they've been meeting up!

There's another brrrrp. Maybe I'm going to get away with this. Maybe Will's not around!

'Hey, Will here, I'm not around at the moment …'

Phew! But hang on – no! Now I'll have to leave a voicemail! A pointless conversation I can get away with ... but a pointless voicemail? That shows real commitment! Commitment to saying nothing!

Beep ...

I remain perfectly quiet. Now he'll never know I rang. I'll just sit here in silence for two minutes and he'll get a blank message and he'll think nothing of it. I stare out of my window, wordlessly.

And then I realise: it rang! His phone rang! I'll be on his missed calls! It'll say I left a message! And now, already, he's got thirty seconds of silence!

'Oh, hi, Will,' I say, casually, as if I'd only just remembered I was supposed to speak. 'Just ringing to say hi.'

More silence. This is dreadful.

'And ... that I'm sorry my car keeps ringing you! Ha ha!'

What else? What else can I say?

'So yeah ...'

Hang up! I think, trying that button again. Hang up!

'Anyway, that's it, really ...'

Outside, a truck overtakes, loudly. That'll *definitely* be on the message.

I sigh.

'It did it again,' I say.

ACTING

I am standing under the head of a dead moose in Los Angeles, about to make my feature film debut.

It is not the way I ever thought I would make my feature film debut. I had assumed that my feature film debut would see me with at least a pistol in my hand, or a glamorous lady on my knee. But no. It is under the head of a dead moose. And I look like a nitwit.

But this is OK. This is *fine*. Because Jim Carrey is standing opposite me, and he's just slapped me on the arm and said, 'How *are* you?'

Jim Carrey has a special nickname for me. It is Braveheart. This is because the first time we met, he referenced my surname and asked me if I was any relation to *William* Wallace, King of the Scots and Knight of Elderslie. Inexplicably, I said yes, and that William Wallace was in fact my dad. I had thought that perhaps we could laugh about this, and bond, and become best friends and walk dogs together, but the moment I'd said it, his assistant had turned up and told him he had to be somewhere else, and now I couldn't help but think that Jim Carrey was under the impression that I genuinely believed my dad was William Wallace, King of the Scots and Knight of Elderslie. He's not. He's *Ian* Wallace, king of the teapots and a man who once spent a night in Elderslie.

Out of embarrassment, I consider naming William Wallace as my father on Wikipedia, just in case Jim Carrey is concerned, and decides to check it out.

My feature film debut is all because of a book I wrote a couple of years ago, called *Yes Man*. It's the story of how I'd been saying

No far too much in life. I'd been staying in, and lying low, and batting away the various invitations that were coming my way. I was hiding out, and claiming I couldn't come over or see that friend or attend that gig because I was … you know … doing a 'thing'. And then everything changed. Because I said Yes.

And now, suddenly, here I was, standing opposite where Jim Carrey had been just before being whisked away, on a Warner Bros. studio lot, with my own huge trailer and an executive by my side. Because *Yes Man* is being made into a film.

'If you're not busy tonight,' says the exec, 'a colleague of mine would like to take you out to dinner … He knows your work very well and would love to ask you about it …'

'Of course!' I say, flattered. 'It would be a *pleasure*!'

It is good being flattered. So long as you don't believe it too much.

The stand-up, Adam Bloom, once told me of his excitement at attending the Montreal Comedy Festival. He had been *spotted*. By an *executive*. This was *it*!

'You were PHENOMENAL!' she bellowed. 'Please! Come to this party tonight! Casey will give you the details … Casey … this is Adam … he was PHENOMENAL!'

Adam turned up at the party, all spick and span, and was pleased when the exec approached him once more. 'You were PHENOMENAL!' she said. A moment later, he overheard her pointing him out to a man with an important face. 'That guy,' she whispered, 'is *phenomenal*!' Adam nearly imploded with joy. Until she returned, five minutes later, with a small plate of crisps in her hand. 'Ohmygod, you have got to try these,' she said. 'They. Are. PHENOMENAL.'

I think Adam left soon after, when he realised they were just Pringles and, as such, not *particularly* phenomenal.

But that won't happen to *me* tonight, I think. After all, *I've* just been filmed under a dead moose.

I arrive at the Chateau Marmont. Terence Stamp has just wandered upstairs. Dawn from *The Office* is talking to a goggle-eyed

Australian. Someone who looks like Ryan Seacrest has just spilt mineral water down his trousers. And the new executive has popped open a bottle of champagne.

'So I have to say,' he says. 'Big fan. *Big* fan.'

Clearly, he thinks I'm more important than I am. Little does he know I was recently bumped from *Celebrity Win, Lose or Draw* in favour of a bloke who hadn't been in *EastEnders* for twenty years.

'There's so *much* to talk about,' he says. 'But mainly, I want to know what it was like … running the *marathon*!'

I smile. And I don't know what to say. Because I have *never* run the marathon.

'You ran the *marathon*, man!' he says, punching me on the shoulder.

'*Did* I?' I say, before correcting myself and saying, 'I *did*?', because I'm in America and sometimes you have to translate.

'Yeah! In, like, *five days*! That's *brave*, man – that's *really brave!*'

I have literally no memory of running the marathon in five days. And surely I should have *five days'* worth. But this man is a *fan* of mine. He *said* so. He *must* be right.

And then I realise. He does *not* love my work. He has just looked me up on Wikipedia. But he has done it incorrectly, and memorised instead the career of the *other* Danny Wallace. The Danny Wallace who played football for Manchester United. The Danny Wallace who had bravely undertaken a torturous and commendable five-day marathon in the name of charity despite suffering from MS. The *better* Danny Wallace. No *wonder* this bloke was a fan.

'I'm not sure that was me,' I say, which is an understatement.

'Yeah, man!' he says. 'I *remember*!'

I shake my head. There is an awkward silence. I have let him down.

'So … you any relation to *William* Wallace?' he finally asks.

'He's my dad,' I say.

And when I get home, I put it into Wikipedia.

FAX

The film company has put me up in a very posh LA hotel. So posh it costs as much to buy a variety pack of cornflakes as it would to buy the entire Kellogg's company. It is fair to say I do not really fit in here, but even so, I am alarmed and concerned by the looks the concierge gives me whenever I walk through reception, carrying my own non-hotel bottles of water and variety packs of cornflakes.

'Does he not know I was once on *Daily Cooks Challenge*?' I ask myself, grumpily, as the lift doors close. 'Does he not know I have met Antony Worrall Thompson?'

I get back to my room and sit down on the bed, thinking of the superior look the man on reception had given me. Why should I be confined to my room through embarrassment? Why should I sit here, feeling awkward and unable to leave?

Ignore it, I think. What can you do?

I fire up the internet and click about. I find my way to Twitter. I consider it. People are *always* on Twitter. Always swapping information. Opinions. Views. And they seem a friendly bunch. What if … what if they could be *mobilised*? Mobilised to help, somehow? Help in gaining the respect of a man whose respect I do not need and would not normally crave?

And then I have an idea: these people could make me look *important*! Convince the man I was some kind of mogul or businessman! Wipe the sneer from his stupid face! They could fax me! Fax me at the hotel! With important messages, such as, 'The Japanese have offered twelve million. What's our next move?'

I tap it out and put it to the people. Their reaction is immediate.

'Fax?' writes one. 'Where are you staying? The 1980s?'

'Come on!' I reply. 'Let's do this! Let us strike a blow for the little man!'

I wait. I wait a little more. And then … the phone rings. It's the man. Apparently there is a fax for me at reception. He's sending it up.

What was that I detected in the man's voice? Could it be reverence and respect? Yes, it could! It's worked!

A knock at my door. A bellboy hands me an envelope. I thank him, very seriously, trying to look harassed and businesslike.

I open it. There are sixteen faxes. *Sixteen!* Take *that*, man downstairs!

I read the first one.

'Spielberg would like to meet you at his office tomorrow to discuss your script.'

Brilliant! Spielberg! Imagine the man's face when he saw that! I read the next ones …

'FAO Danny Wallace. Paramount has greenlit it.'

'Danny – Sweden need to know your response. Call them NOW.'

'Dan. Current offer is just $5 million. Told them to get screwed.'

Ha! And then a knock at the door. It's the bellboy again. He's holding *more* faxes!

'Oh,' I say, and then, with a mysteriously deep voice: 'Thanks.'

I open the envelope, and there are dozens more faxes, but these ones more elaborate, more considered. One has a United Nations letterhead: 'Armenian President Sargsyan requests urgent response. Gold bullion shipment has NOT arrived. Penguins also missing.'

Now there's one from NASA: 'With regards to proposed Apollo 22 mission, NASA has confirmed you will not be alone for the whole duration of the mission. On days 1–13 you will be accompanied by Cheezy the Monkey.'

'Danny! – they have been here – they have taken all the files regarding the transfer – don't use your phone – for God's sake get out of there – trust no one!'

Uh-oh. Perhaps the man might now be having his doubts about me. And they show no sign of stopping. The phone rings again. More faxes are coming up. Still. At least I look interesting. I mean, he might think these are true.

'Universal Genetics' reads the next letterhead. 'Dear Mr Wallace, the results for your paternity test are finally in. Our sincere apologies for the considerable delay caused by the unusual viscosity of your fluids. Congrats, the baby's yours!'

Oh, God! He *might think these are true!*

The faxes continue for some time. I start tipping the bellboy heavily on each visit, as I am accused, variously, of being a spy, a hitman, a convict and a ghost. By the time the last one's in, my floor is covered with more than fifty faxes.

I read the small print in my hotel manual underneath 'Fax Service'. They charge $2 for each incoming fax.

I think about going out to get some food, but realise that would mean walking through reception.

I stay in, and open my variety pack of cornflakes.

CHAMPAGNE

wo days later, I am still in LA, thrilled that my work is done for the day and the city is all mine.

I am alone in this vast and glorious place. My foot is loose. I'm free of fancies.

I can do anything I like!

I could empty the mini-bar! I think, and I open it, wildly, and take out a bottle of champagne. I could drink it dry!

I study the price list and put the champagne back.

Or I could go out! I think. Head for a museum! Or the shops! I could swagger about in LA shops, trying on inappropriate jeans or buying videogames!

I feel the guilty pleasure of the man on a business trip in an exciting city, with time to kill. A man staring out at whole hours free of responsibility. Is there anything better than having nothing to do?

Of course, when my wife phones up, I'll have to complain about how boring it all is, how the room's too small and the bed's too lumpy, how busy I am, how busy I'll *be*, how much she'd *hate* it if she was here. But that is to protect her. To make sure she thinks she's not missing out.

She is, though.

But on what?

I grab a copy of a listings magazine the hotel has put in my room.

Mexican jazz! I think. There's a Mexican jazz gig in town tonight! I could go and watch Mexican jazz!

I start to wonder if I've got time to grow a moustache. I decide I haven't, and that even with nothing to do Mexican jazz might be a step too far, and so I turn the page.

I could go to Universal Studios! I think. Or to the Magic Castle! I could eat at In-N-Out, or maybe I could visit a vineyard and show off that I'm able to tell the difference between red and white wine!

The thought of wine makes me thirsty and I open the mini-bar again. I take out a tiny bottle of wine. I can tell just by looking at it it's white.

Or I could find a great restaurant, I think, as I restudy the price list and then put the bottle back. 'An Afghan one, or an Ethopian deli, or somewhere where I've no idea what I'm ordering, and then I could walk down Venice beach with a taco and buy some rollerskates and pretend I'm in the title sequence of a 1980s American TV show.'

I would love to be in the title sequence of a 1980s American TV show.

Actually, I'd love a taco.

I open the door to the balcony and step outside.

The sun is shining. It's mid-afternoon, but I know the evening won't be far off. I know it's important to act now, because it's *always* important to act now, and time already feels like it's running away, taking with it all the things that I could do on this day of nothing to do.

Maybe I could hire a car, I think, leaning on the railings and staring down at the traffic below. Maybe I could drive out to the valley … or into the desert … or maybe just up to the Hollywood sign …

But I can't decide.

Because suddenly, there is too much to do.

Maybe I'll just stay in the room.

And then, just as I'm switching on the telly and skipping past *17 Again* on the movie options, my phone rings.

It's my wife.

I remember the drill.

I prepare to tell her how boring it all is here, how the room's too small, and the bed's too lumpy, how busy I am and how busy I'll be, how much she'd hate it if she was here, but I don't have the chance, because she's starting to say something, and she's happy, and I can somehow hear the tears in her eyes, and suddenly there's a pause to fill, and she takes a second, and she says, 'I'm pregnant.'

And even ten minutes later, as I've popped the mini-bar champagne, and I've started to scour the internet for flights home, flights right now, flights right this *minute*, I realise I would gladly swap a million nights of anything-I-like and a billion days of nothing-to-do, just to hear her say those words for the first time again.

And indeed, I think I just have.

THE WISDOM AND PHILOSOPHIES OF A MODERN MAN: 3

MONDAY

I met an American man today. He was very jolly indeed, and revelled in telling me jokes. 'What do you do if your girl is peddling her bike all over town?' he said, and I said 'I don't know!' and smiled.

'You take her bike away!'

I didn't really get it, to be honest, but in the name of Anglo-American relations I laughed very hard indeed, and I shook my head at the brilliance of the joke, and then repeated the punchline for effect.

He wandered off, chuckling, and as I was walking away, slightly confused, he ran after me.

'Sorry, man,' he said. 'The joke should be: What do you do if your girl is peddling her BUTT all over town? Take her bike away!'

Now I had to laugh even harder than I had before, and even more hysterically, because this time his joke made sense.

I think I overdid it, to be honest, because he'd started to look at me oddly. I walked away, red-faced and exhausted.

It is very hard being British sometimes.

TUESDAY

I think if you're ever caught in the middle of a bank robbery, a good thing to do would be to compliment the robbers on their choice of disguises, because I bet no one ever thinks to do that, and it takes real guts, walking through town dressed as a clown.

WEDNESDAY

I think it must be really hard to be someone like Richard Reid the shoe bomber, because the next time he's at a dinner party and the conversation turns to jobs, he'll have to say, 'I'm a shoe bomber.' And then everyone will remember who he is, and he'll have to say, 'Look, I've done *other* stuff too, I'm not *just* a shoe bomber,' but all anyone will want to know about is the shoe bombing.

And then, worst of all, he'll know from the looks around the table that everyone will secretly be thinking that he's not even a very *good* shoe bomber, and whoever he was talking to will suddenly change the conversation to what they do, or mortgages.

That is the main reason I would not like to be Richard Reid the shoe bomber.

THURSDAY

I was reading one of those free newspapers on the train this morning and came across the I SAW YOU! column, in which people attempt to woo strangers they've seen on trains but not had the bottle to talk to. One of them said: 'To the scruffy guy in the blue jacket with glasses who was on the Northern Line the other day! Coffee?' I blushed. I had been selected. Noticed. I must've been. How many other men who wear glasses and are scruffy can possibly travel on Europe's busiest transport system? Plus – I own a blue jacket and have been on the Northern Line! This was spooky. But how would I explain this to my wife? I got my phone out in order to prepare a text, as I imagined she'd already seen it and would be distraught. I looked around the carriage, just in case anyone else had spotted this too, and wanted to catch my eye to share the news. There was a scruffy man in glasses sitting opposite me. He was wearing a blue jacket.

We scowled at each other, and then silently put our phones away.

FRIDAY

I attempted to write a stern e-mail today. Stern e-mails aren't something I'm brilliant at, but this stern e-mail had to be stern, so I employed the use of words like 'shocked' and 'vociferous'. The problem was, I'm so used to writing polite e-mails that some of my habits die hard. The end of the e-mail read, 'I expect and demand your full and detailed explanation of these events by the end of the week at the absolute latest. Regards, D. Wallace.'

And then, just after pressing Send, I realised I'd put a little kiss at the end.

SATURDAY

My friend Pete returned to our table at the pub slightly shaken by a man he'd met while standing at the long, trough-like urinals. The man had joined him and grumpily exhaled, before saying, 'There is no way this is a five-man urinal.' It seemed a strange thing to be upset about, as if the pub had been actively promoting the idea of a five-man urinal. Like they'd hung up a sign saying, 'GOOD FOOD! SKY SPORTS! FIVE-MAN URINAL!' Now, however, I find myself assessing urinals in terms of how many men can comfortably stand side by side in front of them, and that is a gift I never thought I'd have.

SUNDAY

I think if you were a soldier under massive artillery attack in the trenches, a funny thing to do would be to pull out a big yellow SuperSoaker and start fighting back with that because, come on, can't we all just be *friends*?

WINTER

PLANS

olin doesn't know it, but his world is about to change for ever. We are in the pub. The same pub in which we have discussed many of the world's most important issues. The same pub which has seen us share our wisdom and impart our philosophies at rough wooden tables with rougher pints of beer for so long now. The pub which has been at the centre of a thousand vital meetings of minds, and a thousand of what Colin likes to refer to as his 'major pub debates'. But tonight, it will be at the centre of something else entirely.

I watch him, as he stumbles inside, the inside of his jacket catching on the door handle, and his surprised face, as if it doesn't happen every time. I continue to watch, as he gives me the thumbs up, does the little shaky 'pint?' gesture with his hand, and then trips as he gets to the bar and tries to choose the crisps.

Ah, sweet, gentle Colin. So innocent. So naïve. So in for a shock.

He sits down, opens his crisps, and immediately senses something is up. Perhaps, as with his cousins in the animal kingdom, he can feel change in the wind.

And so I tell him. I tell him my news. I tell him he's soon to become an honorary uncle. That I'm going to be a dad.

It is fitting I should tell him here, in this pub. Not only is it our regular, but by lunchtime it is the official hangout of each and every mother or mother-to-be in North London. Sometimes you can't move for women breastfeeding. Which is not a sentence I really say very much.

A moment has passed since I told him. And then Colin smiles the broadest smile I've ever seen, and he shakes my hand, and he slaps my shoulder, and he makes a little whooping sound. I smile back, and nod.

And then he looks at me very seriously indeed, and he says, 'You're gonna need a pram.'

I blink once or twice.

That's his first reaction?

I'd thought maybe he'd ask me when it was due, or whether I know what genre it is, or if we'd thought of any names.

'Yep,' he says, taking a sip of his pint. 'You're gonna need a good pram.'

'I … is that your first reaction?' I say. 'Don't you want to know what sex it is?'

'OK. What sex is it?'

'I … don't know.' I shrug, and Colin rolls his eyes at me, as if I've been purposely wasting his time.

'Well, let's refer to it as a "he" for now,' he says, pointing in the air. 'For one thing, it's simpler, and for another, it's very important to remain positive during a pregnancy.'

I nod, confused. Somehow, Colin has taken charge.

'So when it comes to prams,' he says, 'I'd say it was between the Bugaboo and the Maclaren.'

I have never heard of either of these things.

'Of course, there's the Balmoral, but you don't really want to go down that route. Not unless you want your baby picked on by a load of rival babies.'

'*Rival* babies?'

'Yeah. Tough babies. I don't imagine yours is going to be all that tough.'

I am offended. I could have a tough baby if I wanted. What does Colin know about having tough babies? Maybe my baby's a thug! Maybe my baby will be a proper skinhead!

Actually, statistically, it is very likely to be a proper skinhead.

'Now the thing with the Maclaren is it's generally forward-facing and foldable, while the Bugaboo is a fashion statement and generally parent-facing and more minimalist … You're probably tempted by the look of a three-wheeler, but remember that while they're great on rough terrain, they're not so good in the supermarket.'

He realises something and slaps his head to punish himself for forgetting.

'Oh, God! The supermarket!'

'What?' I say, panicking. 'What about the supermarket?'

'Well, what do you go for? Active Fit nappies? Washable cloth? Both have their advantages, yet both are quick to reveal their weaknesses.'

I realise what's happening here. Colin can only deal with a conversation of this magnitude by turning it into a major pub debate.

'Also,' he says, 'we should talk papooses. BabyBjörn is one way to go, but let's not forget the Bushbaby Cocoon …'

He raises his eyebrows at me. I look at him.

'You spend a lot of time here at lunchtimes, don't you?'

'I do, sir!' he says, draining his pint, and looking rather proud. 'I certainly do.'

WIVES

So,' I say to my friends, 'I've invited my pal Steve along.'

We're waiting to be seated in a nice Chinese restaurant where the waiters call you sir. I'm with my wife and another couple, and so far the conversation has included wrestling and Christmas.

And then, from somewhere behind me, I hear him.

'Hey there!'

I turn and there he is, standing proudly, and smiling. He's been waiting in the bar and he's carrying a huge gin and tonic.

'Steve!' I say. 'Hi!'

But he doesn't say anything to me, because he's already hugging my friend's wife, tightly. This is strange. He has never met my friend's wife before.

The hug continues, and he is beaming while he does it. The rest of us fall silent. This really is lasting a little too long. My friend's wife stands stiffly, and I catch Paul looking concerned.

'So *good* to see you!' says Steve, finally releasing her from the hug and then kissing her on the cheek. 'How *are* you?'

'I'm … fine!' she says, a little taken aback.

'How have you been? What are you up to?'

'Oh …' she says. 'Different … things.'

There's a slight lull while Steve still stares into her eyes, grinning.

'Um, Steve,' I say. 'This is Paul.'

He turns and shakes Paul's hand and introduces himself

politely, before turning back to my friend's wife and giving her a matey punch on the arm.

And then, after another awkward silence, he looks at me. And he turns to see who else is here.

And he spots my wife.

My wife. Standing *next* to me.

He glances quickly at my friend's wife, and then back at mine. Something explodes behind his eyes.

'Heeeeey,' he says, biding for time, but I know exactly what's happened. He thought my friend's wife was mine.

They're both little, and they're both brunette, and they both dress the same, but even so, mixing them up is a little embarrassing. Particularly in such a high-energy way. I am the only one to have twigged so far. Paul still stands there, blinking, wondering why this man has been hugging his wife so much and then punching her on the arm.

But I see continued horror in Steve's eyes. Not at what he's done – but at what he now has to *do*. He has set a precedent. Put forward an image. He has bounded in like the most vivacious man the world has ever seen – a man so vivacious he'll hug strangers and stare deep into their eyes – and now, to get away with it, he has to maintain a level of vivacity never before seen in humankind. He has to maintain an unmaintainable level of excitement. He has to be Timmy Mallett.

'C'mere, you!' he suddenly half-yells, grabbing my wife and hugging her like a long-lost sister. He has to show he is *even more* pleased to see her than he was at seeing a stranger, and rattles her about like a rag doll. 'So *good* to see you!'

He catches my eye over her shoulder as he shakes her about and it is clear he is pleading with me not to give the game away. He lets her go and tries to get her to do a high-five, but now *she's* confused too, and possibly dizzy and breathless, and so I complete the high-five on her behalf, and say, 'Let's eat!'

We sit down and attempt polite chit-chat, but the bar has already been set too high. An unwarranted level of intimacy has been established, and Steve now has to act like the life and soul of the party – like a man who *always* walks up to people he's never met before and shouts 'So good to see you!' in their face.

He tells stories. He stands up and acts some of them out. He's loud and brash and has to be especially friendly to Paul so as not to make him think he's after his wife. He joshes with the waiters and uses the chopsticks to make a huge makeshift moustache. And by the end of the meal, exhausted, spent and drunk, he has just about got away with it.

'It was so nice to meet you,' says my friend's wife, as we wait for taxis outside. 'It feels like we've known each other *ages*!'

Steve's cab arrives and I know he can finally relax.

He bids us goodbye and clambers inside.

'Good to see you!' he shouts at the driver, for our benefit. The driver smiles at him and begins a conversation.

It is going to be a long journey home.

THE DREAM

I notice my wife feels a little frosty when I bring her a cup of tea in bed. Perhaps it's hormones. *Pregnancy* hormones. I attempt to find out.

'It's nothing,' she says, waving me away, and I choose to believe her, because it's easier.

But there is still this feeling of slight frostiness as she gets up and puts her clothes on. This is strange. My wife is never frosty. We rarely argue. And yet it really feels like I've done something bad. But still she insists nothing is wrong.

It is only later, as she peers angrily out of the window of a local restaurant, that she reveals the source of her annoyance.

'I had a dream,' she says. 'And in it, you were such a … berk.'

I blink a couple of times.

'A berk?' I say. 'How was I a berk?'

A waitress arrives to take our order. We fall silent and study the menu for a second. But all I can think of is that I've somehow been a berk. A big, nocturnal berk.

'We were in the supermarket,' she seethes, as the waitress disappears to the kitchen. 'And I was just watching you, as you piled carrot after carrot into the shopping trolley. And I was like, "What's with all the carrots?" And you just replied, "I want carrots."'

'"I want carrots"?'

'Yes. That's all you said. "I want carrots." And you just continued to pile them into the trolley. And I said, "That's too many carrots." And you said, "No. I want fourteen carrots."'

'Fourteen?' I say, wondering how I'm going to get out of this one. 'Why did I want fourteen carrots?'

'Aha! Exactly!' she says, like she's finally caught me out and I've admitted it. '*No one* wants fourteen carrots! There is not one recipe in the *world* that requires fourteen carrots!'

'Well, maybe it was *more* than one recipe!' I say, defensively, though I'm not sure why. 'Or maybe I just wanted to nibble on some while I played Xbox. You know I like nibbling on carrots while I play Xbox!'

'You didn't once mention Xbox or nibbling. You just said you wanted fourteen carrots and then continued to pile them into the trolley despite my sensible protestations.'

I struggle to come up with an adequate defence. I have clearly crossed a line here.

'Well, maybe I was planning on surprising you!'

'With fourteen carrots?'

'Yes! And you *spoilt* that surprise! And at least carrots are part of my five-a-day! It could have been worse. It could have been Twixes. Or packets of Wheat Crunchies.'

'It was *carrots*,' she hisses. '*Too many* carrots.'

There is another frosty moment of silence. I look out of the window, hurt, but then I notice a funny dog and everything's OK again.

'And the worst thing was,' she continues, 'the *organic* ones were only in the next section.'

'Eh?'

'I kept saying, "The organic ones are just there!", but oh no, you just kept arrogantly piling the non-organic, bright orange ones into the trolley.'

There is nothing I can say to this.

'I mean, you've got the choice, they're right next to each other, and if you really need that many carrots, at least *some* of them could be organic. I mean, I'm pregnant. I'm eating for two. And organic ones are so much better for the baby.'

I decide she is right. And that I should be the bigger man here. And that I should never refer to my wife as a man.

'I am sorry,' I say, sincerely. 'I shouldn't have bought that many carrots in your dream. And if for whatever crazy reason I *did* need fourteen of them, then at least half, if not all, should absolutely have been organic.'

She looks pleased and melts a little, and after a moment, reaches across the table and squeezes my hand.

Our starters arrive. My wife is having the tomato soup. It looks great. But then I realise something.

'Tomato soup?' I say. 'What did you order for your main, again?'

'Salad,' she says.

'But what kind?'

'Tomato and avocado,' she says, looking at me.

I bristle, and shrug.

'*What?*' she says, icily.

'Just seems like a lot of tomatoes,' I say.

THE ASSISTANT

olin is feeling overworked.

'I had to work all yesterday morning,' he says. 'And then right the way through the afternoon, too.'

'Goodness,' I reply. 'But that's an entire day!'

'Didn't get home until nearly five,' he says, still clearly shocked. I think about it. He can only have had maybe nine, ten hours' sleep.

'It's these people, Dan. They've hired me to work on a project and now they want it done by the end of the week.'

'When did they originally want it done?'

'By the end of the week. But still. I think they're being unreasonable.'

'Yes. Expecting you to work a full day and complete it by the date originally agreed. You're not a *machine*.'

He gives me a 'precisely!' face.

'So I've hatched a plan,' he says.

'Of course you have.'

'I will honour this commitment, Dan. But never will I be led into this trap again. So I'm getting an assistant.'

'You're getting an assistant?'

'Yes. A beautiful one. Russian.'

'Right.'

'Emma Lawrence, the beautiful Russian.'

He says 'Emma Lawrence' again, this time in a Russian accent, but it doesn't really work.

'She will be there for me, Dan, whenever I need her. She will be firm but fair with my clients. She will act as buffer to their crazy demands, and break the news of inevitable delays or damage to them gently.'

'I see.'

'She will be a woman of startling intellect. Taught the works of the great philosophers from an early age by her Nobel-winning father and her supermodel mother, Emma studied the cello at the Sorbonne, and in amongst all her humanitarian work is now looking for a new challenge in life.'

'Working for you in your spare room in North London.'

'*Learning* from me.'

'How will this fictional woman learn from you?'

'Same way you do. And yes, she's fictional, but what of it? Sherlock Holmes was fictional, you like him. Danger Mouse was fictional!'

I wave him on, like he's made his point and brilliantly argued me down.

'I'll just set up an e-mail address,' he says, 'and then write to the clients saying things like, "Colin is in a staff meeting right now" or "Colin has had to fly to New York to close a deal" or "Colin's still in bed". Probably not that last one. Point is, she can be a tough negotiator. Make sure I'm not bullied.'

I consider his idea. It has so much wrong with it that I don't know where to start. So I decide not to start.

'It is an elegant solution, sir!' I say, pompously, and Colin smiles and makes that 'precisely!' face again.

'I just hope you don't have an affair with her,' I say.

'That's the problem,' says Colin, nodding. 'That's the problem.'

The next day, I get a text from him.

'Pub?' it says.

But I am working, and also, it's about five past ten in the morning. I give him a call around six but all I can hear are fruit machines and loud shouting, so I hang up and wait for him to call back. He doesn't.

The following evening, around nine, I get another text.

'Hey, so it's mE an I'm out nabOut.'

I hope this project he's working on is pub-based. If it is, no one can say he didn't put the time in. I start to wonder whether perhaps having an assistant is bad for Colin.

And then the weekend is upon us. We meet for a Sunday roast, and Colin looks shattered.

'Did you get your work done in time?'

'Just. Emma tried to get the deadline extended.'

'What happened?'

'They said no.'

'What did Emma say?'

'Turns out Emma buckles very easily. And also, I think I'll get a male assistant next time. Emma seemed to want to do most of her work from my phone down the pub. A *man* wouldn't want to spend all his time in the pub. I think she's got a problem.'

'You're going to have to let her go.'

'I hate doing stuff like that. That's why I got an assistant.'

'I'll get *my* assistant to do it,' I say, getting my phone out. 'What should we call her?'

PANIC

've been booked to host an awards ceremony 200 miles away from home, and because my baby will need shoes one day, I'm standing in the hotel lobby the evening before. I've just finished checking in when the lady behind reception says, 'And you must try our new Vapour Room. It's a *delight*!'

I nod, and smile broadly, mainly because the lady has used the word 'delight', but I have absolutely no intention of using their new Vapour Room. For one thing, I am tired and hungry, and for another, I don't really know what a Vapour Room is.

Minutes later, my bag is on the floor of a stark and soulless room, with lank, stained curtains, but I am a world away, because I am staring at a laminated pamphlet which shows a woman with a wistful and dreamy gaze on her face. She is lost in a universe of untold pleasure and glowing with health and youth and vigour.

'Visit the Vapour Room,' she seems to be saying. 'You too can look like a vigorous glowing woman!'

I put the pamphlet down.

It must be the vapours, I think. The vapours must be *life-giving*.

And then I decide. I will visit the Vapour Room.

Before I know it, I am in my shorts and striding into the hotel's all-but-abandoned leisure area. I push open the door of the Vapour Room and immediately my glasses steam up with the heat. I take them off, but I don't mind, because this can only be good for me, just as it was for the sweaty, laminated woman.

Well, this is nice, I think, sitting down. When people at the awards ceremony ask me what I did last night, I'll be able to say, 'I visited a Vapour Room,' and they will think me metrosexual and cosmopolitan. 'What happened on *Emmerdale* last night?' they could say, and I will simply shrug and reply, 'I am unsure, as I was in a Vapour Room.'

The closest I have come to this before is Vicks VapoRub, and I'm absolutely sure this is at least a bit better.

The steam is thick, though, and the heat intense, and I wonder whether there's any way of controlling things. I look over to my right, and see the button that must deal with the steam. I take a risk and press it. Nothing happens for a second, and so I press it again, hoping to bring the heat down a little, but still nothing. And then: a small white light appears above it.

I move closer, until my eyes can focus properly, and I read what it says in faint, grey text.

SOS.

Hang on.

SOS?

I have just pressed the SOS button. The SOS button! They're going to think I need help! That I'm passed out or in danger! But I am not! I'm just a bit steamy! What do I do?

I have mere seconds to decide. I do what anyone would do after pressing the SOS button in a Vapour Room. I run outside and jump into the pool.

Oh dear, I think, my shorts full of air. They're going to arrest me. People probably go to jail all the time for causing false alarms in Vapour Rooms!

There is an awful wait, but then, from nowhere, a man in hotel uniform jogs towards the Vapour Room. He casts a concerned glance at me and pushes the door open. He disappears for perhaps five agonising seconds. Then he reappears and looks at me, suspiciously.

I pretend I am relaxing in the pool, and swish my arms around innocently. He waits for a second, and then walks away, grumpily.

Oh God, I think. Why didn't I just tell him? Why didn't I just say, 'I'm so sorry, I pressed the SOS button by accident!' I'm the only person here! He *knows* it must've been me!

I am very angry at myself. Now this man thinks I'm the sort of person who presses SOS buttons and then runs away, which is unfair, because I've only known that myself for about two minutes. Maybe he thinks I do it in disabled toilets, too, just for fun!

Hang on – maybe I *do*! Maybe I'm the sort of person who sets off fire alarms, or lets off extinguishers in the hallways! Just because I've never done it doesn't mean I'm not the sort of person who does it!

I am ashamed of my cowardice. I am an awful human being for not coming clean. I go back to my room and put the healthy glowing woman face down on the table. I do not deserve her gaze. The next time I do something like this, I resolve, I will be upfront. I will be *honest*.

In the morning, at checkout, the lady behind reception asks me if I used the Vapour Room at all last night.

I remember my valuable lesson.

'No,' I say, and I don't bother mentioning it to anyone at the awards ceremony, either.

NAKED

I am standing, cold and half-naked, in a small shower cubicle in North London, opposite a well-built man named Gary, who moments before was a mere stranger.

We are very close indeed.

'OK,' he says. 'Now just pop your trousers off.'

I look at Gary. Gary looks at me. I nod, and do as he says.

Now I am a man wearing only my pants, and I'm trying to look like I'm cool with this, that I'm *always* standing in small shower cubicles wearing just my pants with well-built strangers named Gary … but then I realise that this is probably the *wrong* impression to be giving at this time, and so I look at my watch, which I discover I'm not wearing.

Gary kneels down and reaches around my waist with his big, burly arms.

Well, I think. *This* is an awkward situation for a man.

'OK,' says Gary, who I've just realised deserves his anonymity, so let's call him Barry. 'Those are your measurements done.'

He puts the tape down.

'Let's get on with it!'

Barry is my brand-new personal trainer. I don't imagine that's his only job – he probably trains *other* people, too – but today he is mine, and it's his mission and duty to recondition my tired and aching body. I have never been any good at exercise. I have always been very *bad* at it. But maybe this will change things.

Hopefully, I think, this will not take much more than a day.

My decision to employ Barry was not one I saw coming. But lately, something's been ... changing. I mean, in the past, I've heard fellow gentlemen talk about looking in the mirror, at their slight paunch or their slowly retreating hairline, and thinking, Well, this is it ... this is literally the best I will ever look, and then giving up on life and buying jeans with drawcord waists and a trowel. And I've talked to *other* men – men just two or three years older than me – who've stared at me in shock and disgusted disbelief and said, 'What do you *mean*, you don't have a "takeaway night"? What do you *mean* you just have them *unplanned*?'

But none of this seemed to relate to me in any way. Not until last week. Last week, when I passed a billboard shouting about a 'Revolution' in 'Personal Training!' Last week, when I stood in the rain and stared at it. Last week, when I stared at the Big Mac, damp in my hands, and wondered whether something had to give.

Last week, when I turned a year older.

'Well done, mate!' I hear, suddenly. It's Barry, who I think I'll start calling Gary again. 'Well *done*!'

Gary seems delighted at my progress. Already, I have done ten sit-ups, and later, I plan to do an eleventh. We move to the weights, and I seem to be very good at those, too, and Gary claps his hands together, and says 'Well done!' From nowhere, I am filled with a manly enthusiasm for the task ahead. Why didn't I do this years ago?

Unless ... no.

Gary does not seem the type to say 'well done' to *everyone*. In his job, you've got to shape up or ship out, and it doesn't pay to encourage the ones with no natural talent for these things. Gary told me well done on the rowing machine, too, so it seems I'm great at rowing, and now that I'm on the treadmill, he seems *more* than quietly impressed.

'Excellent work,' he tells me, as I replace *literally* the first dumbbells I have ever touched. 'Really *well done*.'

We high-five and then he shakes my hand. We stare at each other meaningfully for a second, and then I remember he's seen me in my pants, and I pretend to be distracted by a fly.

But I am *proud* of myself.

I hand Gary my credit card to pay for the session, but he fumbles it and it drops to the floor. I reach down to pick it up.

'Well done, mate,' he says. 'Well done.'

He sticks the card in the Chip and Pin machine and I start to feel uneasy. We wait in silence for a second and I think about what he's just said. I wonder just how well I managed to pick that up. Was it *really* worth a well done?

'Just your Pin number, please,' he says, and I tap it in.

He stares at the screen. I stare at him. The payment goes through.

'Well done,' he says.

On the way home, I buy a Big Mac.

THE INVITATION

The mail has arrived and I stare at it, bleary-eyed and tea-stained. Something from British Gas, I think. Maybe an invitation to a party, or a letter telling me they like me. I ignore it, and flick to the next one.

Something from the council, I think. Maybe an invitation to a party, or a letter telling me they like me.

I flick to the next.

And I stare at it.

Because there is something very odd about this letter.

I turn and scuttle upstairs to find my wife.

'Hey!' I say. 'I've got a letter!'

'That's nice,' she says, also bleary-eyed. 'Who's it from?'

I turn the envelope around and she stares at it.

'What does it *say*?' she demands.

'I don't know!' I say. 'I haven't *opened* it!'

'*Open* it!'

I pause, and look again at the address printed along the back. It says 10 Downing Street.

'What do they *want*?' I say, panicked. 'What have I *done*?'

I think back to the week before, when I'd waved at a speed camera in a cheeky manner. I hadn't been speeding at the time, but what if there was a *law* against waving at a speed camera in a cheeky manner? What if somehow *Gordon Brown* had found out about my cheeky wave? What if this was his particular bugbear? What if he'd only ever been voted in as an MP in the *first* place thanks to his no-nonsense stance on people who wave at speed cameras in cheeky manners?

'Open it!' demands my wife, again. And so I frown, and take a deep breath, and I do.

Ten seconds later, I stare at her gravely.

'I have been *chosen*!' I say.

'For what?'

'For ... a *task force*!'

She grabs the letter and reads it. I have been invited by Prime Minister Gordon Brown to take part in a private, early-morning discussion about science and its place in our future. It is very select, and those chosen to participate handpicked for their unique knowledge and abilities. Clearly, there is some kind of threat to the earth's future. Perhaps a meteorite! Hence the urgent task force!

'It doesn't say "task force" here,' says my wife, which is typical. 'It says "discussion".'

'Oh, come on! It's a *task* force! Gordon Brown is assembling a task force and he wants *me* to be *in it*! There's clearly a meteorite!'

'The phrase "task force" is literally never once mentioned,' she says. 'But a "discussion" is good! You're going to have a *discussion* with the *Prime Minister*!'

It's a *task force*, I think. Women are terrible at reading between the lines.

'So what are you going to do?' she says. 'What are you going to *wear*?'

'A suit!' I say. 'I'm moving in different circles now! I'll be hobnobbing at Downing Street with the nation's top boffins! Maybe *I'm* a boffin! Maybe *that's* why Gordon Brown has chosen me to be in his A-Team!'

'Again, it never once mentions an "A-Team".'

'It doesn't have to! Gordon knows we read between the lines!'

'Boffins?'

'Men!'

I choose which suit to send to the dry cleaners and I e-mail my RSVP.

As I await further instructions, I ponder why Gordon sees *me* as the key to taking science into the twenty-first century. Hey – not just *that*: maybe even *saving the world!*

'He probably saw that episode of *Horizon* I presented recently,' I consider. 'He probably decided there and then he needed my help. That is why we're to have this private discussion at Downing Street. That, and the meteorite.'

I make a pompous face and pick up the suit I've chosen for the dry cleaners.

But who else will be there? I wonder. It can't simply be me and Gordon. We'll get nothing done! I only got a C for GCSE science, and while he's good at maths, that's not quite enough to save the world, is it?

I decide that Hawking will probably bumble in at some point, and I try and think of some other famous scientists, but all I can think of is Newton, and I've not heard about him in *ages*.

And then an e-mail arrives.

'Have you had your suit dry-cleaned?' asks my wife, later. 'And how about Downing Street? Have you heard who else will be there?'

I nod.

'Well?' she says. 'Who else is in this "task force"?'

I am pleased she is finally calling it a task force, but can't help but feel I'm about to let her down.

'Well, it's me ...' I say, 'Tim Lovejoy ...'

She smiles, encouragingly.

'... and Jon Tickle from *Big Brother 4*.'

She tries to make an impressed face, but secretly, we both know that this is not a task force. Although on the plus side, the world is *not* about to be destroyed by a meteorite, because even if

I were prime minister, I wouldn't expect me, Tim Lovejoy and Jon Tickle to sort it out.

I put my suit on, and I go anyway. I arrive at 7.30 on the dot and quickly text my wife.

'You stink!' I write.

It's an in-joke, dating back a few years, when I'd decided to text my mum the very same thing, just to see how she'd react. But there's no instant reply, so I turn my phone off, I take a deep breath, and I knock on the door.

Inside Number 10, I find a coffee and pat Jon Tickle on the back. He turns a little too quickly and spills my coffee on the Downing Street carpet.

'Well, looks like I've made my "mark" on history!' I say, which was very clever of me, but Tickle's not listening, because he's looking at his notes.

'You've got notes?' I say. 'How come you've got notes? Were we supposed to bring notes?'

'Just a few salient points to raise,' says Tickle, and suddenly Lovejoy's there.

'How come every time the world's in danger, they call on *us* three?' I say, but Lovejoy's not listening either, because as it turns out, it's *not* just us three – it's Attenborough, Bryson and Pratchett as well. How am I supposed to compete with that lot?

And then a door swings open and the Prime Minister walks in. He pauses for a moment to say hello to Heston Blumenthal, who's also appeared, and says something important to Hugh Fearnley-Whittingstall. And then he fixes his eyes on me and Jon Tickle, and strides over, hand out.

'Thank you,' he says, sincerely, and shaking my hand, 'for *all* your hard work.'

I look at him, confused.

'Not at all,' I say. 'It's been a pleasure.'

And he's gone again.

'All my hard work?' I whisper, to Jon. 'I've not *done* anything yet. Or does he mean on things like *Richard & Judy*? Is *that* what he's thanking me for?'

But we will never know, because we are called in for our very important meeting.

Inside, I am sitting next to Bill Bryson and trying to make myself look more intelligent than I am. I touch the side of my glasses from time to time, just so everyone can see I'm wearing glasses, and so will assume I am probably a great thinker. Around me, people are talking passionately about science and its place in our country. Jimmy from *Jimmy's Farm* raises some good points, and Charlie Boorman insists it should all start in the classroom. Tim Lovejoy remains tight-lipped, possibly wondering how to turn the conversation round to football. I am still waiting for someone to reveal the *real* reason we are all gathered here – the island full of dinosaurs or the alien crash site – but everyone seems fine just discussing science. Maybe it wasn't a cover after all.

And then, suddenly, it is my turn to speak. All eyes turn to me. And I begin to talk. And talk. And I end up talking about a drunk Brazilian man I met in an East London bar the previous Saturday at 2am.

There is a pause.

The conversation moves on.

I write a note on my special Downing Street notepaper and pass it to Bryson.

'I sounded like a nitwit,' it says, 'but I think I got away with it.'

He chuckles, and writes a reply.

'I *am* a nitwit, and I *always* get away with it,' it says.

I chuckle back and we both stare at the words.

And then Bill scribbles it out, perhaps realising that wouldn't be the best thing to leave on a table if Gordon decided to suddenly check our notes.

I leave Number 10 and stand on a near-deserted Downing Street. A friendly policeman offers to take a picture for me. So I switch on my phone and set it to 'camera', and while he's finding the right shot, I think about my morning.

Not too bad, I consider. I did not embarrass myself. Apart from the coffee incident, and the story about the drunk Brazilian.

'Ready?' says the policeman, but then the phone makes a ding-ding noise.

A text.

'Oh,' says the policeman, looking concerned. 'What's this?'

I look at the screen. It's a reply from my wife. It says, 'Tell Gordon he stinks!'

I consider explaining, but just have my photo taken and leave.

THE BISHOP

I am surfing the internet late at night when I stumble across an unkind comment someone has made about a friend of mine. The friend in question is a broadcaster, but I know him as a kind and generous man, who is funny, and enthusiastic, and warm.

I am startled by the comment, which implies he is silly and lightweight and not worthy of his status as a celebrated breakfast broadcaster and social commentator.

At first, I click away, wishing the internet wasn't like this, jam-packed full of people throwing out highly charged opinions they don't really hold in the real world, making themselves more pompous and opinionated on-line. They're just showing off, I tell myself, and being anonymous helps, too. Who are these people who post nasty things anonymously, or make up names and leave dodgy comments? They're angry souls, or teenage girls, point-lessly squabbling about celebrities.

And then I click back one more time, and I notice that this has not been posted anonymously. It is not an angry soul, or a teenage girl.

It is a bishop.

A *bishop*! An ordained or consecrated member of the Christian clergy! A member of society entrusted with a position of author-ity and oversight! A potential *pope*!

What's a potential *pope* doing listening to my friend in the shower? Why's he writing not very nice things on his blog? Why would he do that? Are bishops not busy enough, doing the things that bishops do? Is this bishop, as a practising friend of Jesus, merely passing on the *son of God's* opinions about my pal? Do *all* bishops feel this way?

And can I really raise a child in a world where all bishops feel this way?

I want to phone my friend and console him, but how do you do that? What do you say? 'I'm sorry to hear that you're not popular with bishops'? But what if that affected his broadcasting? What if every time he opened his mouth to talk about foxhunting or a new survey about Britain's favourite fruit, he was distracted by the fact that somewhere in Britain, a big-hatted bishop was furiously slamming his fists down on his breakfast table, or making sarcastic comments about him to Mrs Bishop, or drawing silly pictures of him and holding them up at sermons?

I cannot tell him.

So I do what a friend would do. I make up a name and post on the blog.

'Hello Bishop,' I start. 'Your comments about ******* aren't very Christian.'

I think for a second, and tap my chin, and work out how to finish.

'But I forgive you.'

I feel the bishop will like this. I am showing the understanding and humanity he will doubtless approve of. I click 'Post' and feel instantly better. I have said my piece. I can move on with my life.

But now I start to worry. I have contradicted a bishop. He was only giving his opinion. And the rest of his blog was very good. It was forward-thinking, and personable, and just the way the church should be. I start to worry that I have jeopardised any chance I would have had of *finally* attaining a sainthood. What if he sets a pack of priests on me?

I see my friend that night, and we have a quiet pint in North London. He insists on paying. I smile, and remember the blog. How could anyone write such things about a man who would not only buy another man a pint, but who would offer you some of his Twiglets, too? Is that not what Jesus would do with a packet of Twiglets, if Jesus really loved Twiglets?

When I get home, warmed by lager, I cannot resist. I check the bishop's blog once more. He has replied.

'Thank you for your input,' he says, which I am pleased about. 'But if I had written anything that was not correct, you might be right in your conjecture.'

I am outraged! Not correct? *Might* be right? He is *standing by* his statement! He is saying it is the truth! Not just his *opinion* – but the *truth*! What if he also thought it was the Way and the *Light*? That could *really* hurt my friend's career!

I must resist the urge to read on. I must turn the other cheek. But I don't. 'If you are offended,' he continues, 'then I am very sorry for telling the truth.'

That was not an apology!, I think, shaking my head. *Clever bishop!*

And then I realise. I am a teenage girl. And so is the bishop. We are just two teenage girls pointlessly squabbling about celebrities. I don't want to be a teenage girl, pointlessly squabbling with a bishop. I only had myself to blame. *I'd* written 'I forgive you', which was cheeky, but *he'd* started it, by picking on my mate. And then we'd both sat at our computers – a grown man and a potential pope – waiting for the other to respond.

I realise the bishop and me are never going to agree. I post again, feebly telling him he'd not really apologised, but insisting he enjoys his tea. He posts back, jokily challenging me to a duel.

I meet up with my friend and tell him that I've been involved in a dispute concerning him. A dispute that never would've happened in the real world. A dispute between me and a bishop.

'Ha,' he says, not in the least concerned. 'That's bishops for you.'

I walk home, and I realise, no: that's the *internet* for you.

I decide not to log on when I get back.

I pass a church, and I walk a little quicker.

THE SCAN

My first cup of coffee is a large one. It's early in the morning and we're at the clinic where we'll be able to see a baby scan of our upcoming release.

Other soon-to-be parents wander around, as clueless as us, and we smile at them and nod, the same way people who own VW campervans flash their lights at each other when they pass.

But not everything's perfect. Just minutes ago I walked past a room marked 'Sluicing Chamber' and now I can't eat my muffin. I don't know what a Sluicing Chamber is or what it is that needs sluicing but early in the morning is no time to be thinking about it, and a muffin doesn't taste the same once someone's pointed it out.

We sit in our chairs and stare at the wall.

'Exciting, though!' I say to my wife. 'Seeing how he's developing! Imagine if he's wearing the same clothes as me! Or if he's already got a little moustache. Or if it's a *she*, and *she's* got one. That'd be weird.'

'It *would* be weird,' replies my wife, looking at her phone. 'It would be *very* weird.'

'Do you think one day a woman will be born who will really suit a moustache?' I say.

Weirdly, it seems my wife isn't really listening.

Downstairs, ten minutes later, everyone is very serious, as the lady with the machine slathers gel on to my wife's tummy.

'I was just saying,' I say, a wry smile on my face, because these people *love* a bit of baby humour. 'Wouldn't it be weird if the baby had a moustache? And a little pipe, say.'

The lady doesn't look at me, but says, 'That would be cause for concern, yes.'

And then she reaches for the magic wand that'll help us see inside.

And it is incredible.

'Wow,' I say.

'Wow,' says my wife.

'Hello!' I try, but the baby seems to take after my wife, and isn't really listening. 'That's ... *wow* ...'

'There's Baby!' says the lady.

'It looks ...' I try and find the right words, the special words that will mark this occasion for ever. '... like the weirdest little alien!'

My wife smiles but the lady doesn't.

'It looks *beautiful*,' she says.

'Yes!' I say, and thinking about it, that would have been better. 'A *beautiful* alien, I mean. Like ET. Not like the Predator, or anything. That would be a worry, if it looked like the Predator. *That* would be cause for concern. But *our* one looks like a beautiful ET.'

No one says anything for a bit.

'Now, Baby's the wrong way up at the minute,' says the lady. 'But they know what to do. Baby will turn itself around in good time. No good it coming out legs first!'

My wife laughs, and so do I.

'That'd hurt!' she says, and we all laugh again. This is nice.

'Of course,' I say, squeezing my wife's hand. 'Sometimes they come out sideways ...'

The lady puts her magic wand away and looks at us, very seriously.

'They do *not* come out sideways,' she says, and then turns to my wife. 'Please, do not worry about that. Baby will take care of it.'

I find it weird the way the lady keeps calling the baby 'Baby'. Like that's its name. She hasn't mentioned *my* name yet. Maybe she just calls me 'Man'.

And then it's over, and we take our printouts and leave.

Upstairs, as my wife stares at the photos, smiling, we pass a small child who's playing with a doll, in among a mass of stuffed animals.

I lean down.

'Nobody puts Baby in the fauna,' I say, and I chuckle and look around, to see if anyone's noticed how clever I've been, but no one has, and now the child is looking at me like he hates me. Children don't appreciate wordplay. And some of the new ones just don't get 80s film references, either.

Outside, I finish my large coffee and throw the cup in a bin, and my wife casually remarks, 'Oh, by the way, the lady in there, she said you don't need to come to *all* the scans. Not if you don't want to. If you're, you know, busy.'

Which is weird, because I'd been there the whole time, and I don't remember anyone saying that at any point whatsoever.

I suppose this is what you'd call a mother's intuition.

'I fancy a muffin,' I say.

CANCELLATIONS

t is 4.38 on a freezing Sunday morning and I am tired and drunk. Colin and I have been sitting in my front room, glassy-eyed and barely speaking, for the past forty-five minutes, waiting for his cab. A cab that has told us – twice – that it's just 'a couple of minutes away'.

Each time I believed the controller. Each time I said 'Thanks!' and hung up. But he has let us down. He has lied to us. The controller is taking us for fools.

I pick up the phone once again and dial.

'Cab service?'

'Um, hi. It's me again. You're picking my friend up, and ...'

'Yeah, he's two minutes away, mate ...'

'But is he *really*?' I say, bravely. 'Because you've said that a couple of times, and ...'

'Swear to God.'

And he hangs up on me.

I put the phone down. And I look out of the window. And I watch absolutely nothing occur for two minutes. And I realise that this *always* happens to me. And that this *always* happens to my *friends*. And that life shouldn't *be* like this. People should make *good* on their promises. People should provide a decent service. And other people should demand they should. We should *rise up*!

And I am filled with a sudden and unexpected rage. I pace to the phone, pick it up and dial the number. I know how to find happiness.

'Cab service?'

'That's what *you* call it!' I say, my voice indignant and my finger in the air. 'What *I* call it is another matter!' I am rising up!

'Did you want a cab, mate?'

'Yes, I did. Forty-five minutes ago.'

'Oh, yeah, he's just around the corner ...'

'No, he's *not*!' I say. 'If he *was*, he'd be *here* by now! It's 4.40am! On a Sunday! How busy can you be at 4.40am on a Sunday?'

'Well ...'

'No! *Not* well! I am phoning merely as a courtesy to inform you that I am *cancelling* this cab, sir!'

Colin looks up at me. He looks strangely proud of me. I am *happy*.

'And what's more ...' I say, my fingers tingling with the electricity of the moment, 'I am cancelling ALL FUTURE CABS!'

Colin looks shocked. So do I. I have no idea where that came from. *What* future cabs? I have *no* future cabs booked! I have no *account* with these people! I don't even think they *do* accounts! And yet I feel ... *powerful*!

'Wait,' says the man. 'We can work this out!'

'NO!' I shout. 'You've *had* your chance! ALL FUTURE CABS ARE NOW *CANCELLED*!'

I slam the phone down. I am high on power. I have especially enjoyed the sweeping arm movements I've been employing when shouting 'CANCELLED!' I dial another number. Three minutes later there's a cab at my door.

'Night,' mutters Colin, stumbling into it, but I know what he means. He means: 'What madness have I witnessed here? Will things ever be the same in our world?'

Well, no, Colin, they will not. Because Colin has witnessed me taking charge. Taking *control*. Steering my own destiny! *Why do I not complain more?* I think to myself in the shower, hours later. *I should definitely complain more!* I'd never realised ... but complaining makes you *happy*.

It is the evening. My takeaway has arrived twenty minutes after the promised forty had expired. I sternly inform the delivery driver that he is to mention this to his superiors. The delivery driver looks at me with respect in his eyes. In me, he sees a man taking control. We nod silently at each other for a second and then I close the door.

My Chicken Madras is lukewarm and dry. The rice is oily. My poppadoms smashed and broken. I do my best to munch my way through it, before the rage is back. The *indignant* rage. I rise up!

'My Madras is dry, my rice is oily and my poppadoms are shattered!' I yell down the phone. 'Shattered like the hopes and dreams I had of a lovely curry!'

'Sir, I do apologise,' says the man. 'If ...'

'No! There will be no "ifs" today! I want *no* refund from you! I want no *replacements*! I want simply to tell you that this was a *bad* curry, sir! A curry so *bad* –' I get ready to employ my sweeping arm gesture '– that I am CANCELLING *ALL FUTURE CURRIES*!'

'We will look after you!' says the man, desperately. 'If you ...'

'NO! NO MORE CURRIES! I HAVE CANCELLED THEM ALL!'

By the end of the following day, I have cancelled all future prawns. The Northern Line is dead to me. I've boycotted Netto and Superdrug. And never again will I eat a McNugget.

I have risen up! I have made my stand! But I catch sight of myself in the window of a passing bus. I look ... *sad*.

When I get home, I order a curry. It's twenty minutes late.

I tip, and I tip heavily.

THE DOODLE

'm back in LA for work, and find myself in a restaurant halfway down a canyon. Around me are the great and the good of the city. It's a beautiful place, with an outdoor patio draped in velvet, but instead of tablecloths there's brown paper, and in the middle of the table a small glass full of crayons.

It's a little odd, but I decide to say nothing. I would hate to expose myself as the only person in the world not aware of this new brown-paper-tablecloth and free-glass-of-crayons eating experience.

The people I'm with are important, and wearing suits.

'This place,' says the first important person. 'It has the best dessert. To die for. Only reason I come here ...'

She laughs, lightly, and I join in, and then we talk about the economy, and the best place to buy pizza, and about driving cars off little ledges. But eventually, I can take it no more.

'So these crayons,' I say. 'What are they for?'

'Oh, they're in case you're feeling arty,' says the second important person. 'You might need to express yourself. This is a restaurant that encourages freedom of expression ...'

He takes a crayon – a yellow one – and starts to doodle. He draws a little house, and we all agree on how brilliant it is.

Soon, all three of us have crayons, and we start to doodle while we wait for our food. It is a bit like being in a creche, except in a canyon, and where the other toddlers wear suits. A 1920s creche, maybe, although that doesn't really explain the canyon.

'So, you missing home?' says the first important person, as I continue my doodle of interesting swirls and vital shapes. 'You're having a kid soon, right?'

'Yes,' I say, proudly, and suddenly I am a little homesick, halfway down this canyon. My doodling becomes more maudlin, and I switch to dark blue.

'Your life's about to change, buddy,' says the second important person, and I immediately think about what a shame it is more people don't say 'buddy'. 'Time to grow up. You won't know what's hit you …'

I continue absentmindedly doodling, my thoughts elsewhere, back home, and the man continues.

'Soon as that little guy pops out, your world is about responsibility …'

I switch to a black crayon – a crayon as black as the night, as dark as the word 'responsibility' – and start to fill in some of the shapes.

'You can forget about going out,' he says. 'You can forget about sleep …'

And then I catch a strange look from the first important person. It's only for a split-second, and then gone again, as she quickly grabs her wine glass and looks away. Maybe I zoned out. Maybe I was lost a little too long. Maybe I looked rude. And then I see it.

From her angle, it would appear I have absentmindedly drawn a childish representation of a lady's nonsense.

Yes. A lady's *nonsense*.

I panic, and immediately start to change it. I didn't mean to do this. I didn't mean to draw a lady's upside-down nonsense. I was just drawing shapes! But I have to change it! So I add a wild red circle around it, but that only seems to highlight what I've done, so I add little wings and turn it into a butterfly. I start to hum, as if I'm casual and calm, but for goodness' sake, I've just inadvertently drawn a lady's nonsense on a table in a fancy restaurant.

This was an accident – a coincidence – but this also is the kind of thing far-reaching psychotherapy papers are based on. I was only drawing shapes! Shapes and other shapes! But somehow those shapes conspired against me and made me not only draw a lady's nonsense, but somehow angle it straight at a lady! And all while talking about my unborn child!

She looks back after a moment or two, and to give me the benefit of the doubt, says, 'So what have you drawn?'

I freeze.

'Just … a butterfly. A mad butterfly.'

She says nothing. I grab a purple crayon and start to scribble it out.

'Killing it,' I say, jokily, but then I bristle, because now I sound like a psychopath with woman issues.

We start to talk about the economy again, but no one's very interested, and I can't help but notice that at the end of the meal, no one seems all that keen to order dessert.

TYPECAST

An exciting e-mail has arrived from a man I've only ever briefly met.

'Would you like to be in a videogame?' it reads.

A videogame! Me, playing a character in a videogame!

'There's one part I think you'd be absolutely *perfect* for! Up for it?'

'Yes I am!' I write back. 'Let's *do* this!'

And then he writes back and tells me not to get ahead of myself, as he'll need to audition me, and they're seeing other people, and it's still early days, and it's not solely his decision, but, y'know, good luck.

I turn up to a small room in Soho, and the man is pleased to see me.

'It's a pretty easy part,' he says. 'It could have been written for you. I think my advice is, just be yourself.'

I nod, eagerly, and he hands me a wad of paper. A script!

'There's a page near the front which explains the characteristics we're after,' he says, and he leaves as I sit down with a coffee to prepare.

This is exciting, I think, opening the document. Welcome to the world of the thespian! Welcome to life … as an *actor*.

And then I read the list of character traits. The list of traits which I – out of 60 million people – have been specially selected to personify.

And then I frown. And I read them again.

Awkward. Nerdy. Lonely. Intense. Contrary.

Eh?

I think back to the man's words.

'It could have been written for you … one part you'd be perfect for … just be yourself …'

I balk slightly. Is this man saying I am awkward, nerdy, lonely, intense and contrary? Or merely that I *seem* awkward, nerdy, lonely, intense and contrary?

I suddenly feel quite awkward, and all alone in the world. But then I realise I'm obsessing over the list too much, so decide to fully concentrate instead on learning my lines.

Like a nerd.

Like a lonely, intense, awkward nerd.

Oh my God. He is right.

'Ready for you now, Dan,' says the man, poking his head round the door. I stand, and attempt to pick up my bag and fling the strap over my head in one sweeping movement, but the strap catches my glasses and I say 'Ow' loudly.

The man smiles and leans against the doorframe as I sort myself out. The smile annoys me. He clearly thought that was both awkward and nerdy.

I decide to use my 'cool' walk to get me across the room – the one I use when I'm walking towards groups of youths to make them think I'm probably quite tough and thinking about Kanye or punching bears instead of worrying about getting mugged – but by the time I've instigated it I'm already at the door, so I abandon it, which just looks odd.

'Danny, this is Peter,' says the first man, and I shake hands with Peter. I catch him checking out what I'm wearing. It's a cardigan. Christ, I'm playing right into these people's hands.

'OK, so in your own time, please …' says Peter, and I begin to read my lines. But as I do, I realise something. I am not performing the words in the way they want. I am not doing them in a nerdy, awkward way. I am doing them in what I imagine is a hip, happening way. I am doing them in precisely the opposite way they want. So incensed am I by being branded awkward, lonely, nerdy, intense and contrary that I would rather not get this part than have them think I am any of those things.

'OK ...' says Peter. 'And once more, maybe?'

I start again, but I begin to improvise this time, changing certain words and phrases to make me seem more urban and streetwise, like at any moment I might do a fingersnap and start downloading something. It seems I am actively trying not to get a job I actually want.

Oh God. I am being contrary.

Peter looks at the first man, who casts an apologetic look back.

'I guess I should just say again,' says the first man, 'that I think this'll work a lot better if you just ... be yourself.'

I buckle under the pressure. I read the words as myself.

I am furious when I get the part.

SHISHAS

am standing in the airport holding a three-foot metal shisha. The kind you see old men in films smoking unusual tobaccos from, inside tents in Middle Eastern villages.

My friend Wag is standing next to me, also holding a three-foot metal shisha.

'That was nice of them,' I say. 'To give us both these big shishas.'

'It was,' says Wag. 'It was *very* nice of them.'

We look at our suitcases, and then at our backpacks, and then at our little carrier bags full of water and chewing gum. We look at our huge and cumbersome shishas again. It is four o'clock in the morning and the last thing we need is huge and cumbersome shishas.

'So … we're going to take these shishas all the way back to England, are we?' says Wag.

I nod, because it is the right thing to do, and so does Wag, and we both pretend it was a very normal thing to say, and that there was no subtext there whatsoever. Why *wouldn't* we take these shishas all the way back to England? They were, after all, a kind and generous gift from some kind and generous people who'd been showing us around their lovely country – and who *doesn't* take a gift home with them? Rude people, that's who. *Ungrateful* people. And we are neither.

We inch forward in the queue towards security. We move our suitcases. Our backpacks. Our little carrier bags. And then we look at each other and shift our shishas, too.

The main problem, I decide, as I look at Wag, is that carrying a shisha around an airport makes you look like a drug-obsessed tourist intent on using his shisha for illegal means. Plus, we look like those sunburnt men you see shouting their way through airports who leave a vapour trail of Kouros and Ouzo, and cradle straw donkeys and wear sombreros and have specially made T-shirts with names on them, like Titty, and Biff.

Oh, God. We're Titty and Biff.

The men at security eye us suspiciously, but allow us through, and we grapple with our shishas and move, like pack horses, through the airport. We've been given free passes to the first class lounge, even though we are most definitely *not* travelling first class, and we drag our stuff inside. The lounge is like someone's ... well ... lounge. Small and poky and with a sleeping man in the corner.

He wakes up.

'Hello!' he says. 'Coffee? Coca?'

We smile and put our shishas down, and grab a coffee and a pastry each, and soon the uniformed man nods off again. Our flight is in an hour, but it can't come soon enough. We are coasting on an hour's sleep, still lightly drunk from late-night gins on a warm hotel balcony.

On a small TV in the corner, Mr Bean tries to open a jar. Wag starts to laugh, and then I start to laugh, and before long we are two sleep-deprived, laughing idiots, unable to control ourselves. The sleeping man wakes up. We try to stop our giggling but we can't. We are now giggling *because* we are giggling.

'So ...' he says. 'You have shisha!'

'Yes,' I say.

'*Nice* shisha,' he says, smiling.

'They were gifts,' I say. 'Lovely gifts.'

'You can smoke *hashish*!' he says, which is surprising, and then he laughs like he was joking, and we laugh politely, and we shake our heads and say 'no!', and then he laughs some more like he was *definitely* only joking, and then he says ... 'You *want* some?'

It is an awkward moment. We are being offered drugs by a man who works in the first class lounge of an airport. What do you say to that? What if it's a local *custom*? I try hard, but I can remember nothing of the sort being mentioned in the Rough Guide.

'Um ... we're OK, thanks,' I say, and he says 'No?' and smiles, and Wag pipes up and says, 'Thanks for the offer, though.'

The man wanders off, sits down and shuts his eyes again.

'Wag, these things are giving us reputations,' I whisper. 'You can't giggle near a shisha! Imagine what they'll think at customs when we get back to London! They'll think we're drugs mules! Or *barons*!'

'I'd rather be a drugs baron than a drugs mule,' says Wag, thoughtfully. 'I imagine the hours are better.'

We decide there and then that we'll have to lose the shishas. We lay them by the sofas in the lounge and wait for the man to nod off. We pick up our backpacks and carrier bags and begin to creep out ... and then we *run*.

We *make* it. We get to the gate and board our plane. But we're feeling guilty for leaving our gifts behind.

'We had to,' I say to Wag, shaking my head seriously. 'We had to.'

The plane is ready to go. We are free. But then there is some kind of kerfuffle near the front. Raised voices. A foreign language. And then a steward strides down the gangway, holding two massive shishas.

'You forgot your shishas in the lounge!' he says, very loudly.

People turn to look at us. They assume we are so stoned we forgot our own implements. We smile politely as the steward stows them above us, and then he gives us a conspiratorial wink, as if to say, 'I know what *you* two are up to ...'

On the way home, we decide that if anyone asks, Wag can be Titty, and I will be Biff.

WORRY

As they get older, it seems many men tend to find concern in the idea that they are turning into their fathers.

I am concerned I may be turning into my mother.

As my wife grows her perfect baby-sized bump, I find myself becoming increasingly worried about the dangers of modern-day life. Dangers I never saw before. But there is danger *everywhere* now.

Cars. Stairs. Parks. Ice. Shoelaces. All of them *deathtraps*.

My Lord. I'm even using the word *deathtrap*.

My mum knows all about danger. As I grew up, this once carefree and footloose Swiss woman could suddenly see potential accidents and terrible occurrences everywhere. No matter how unlikely, no matter how infinitesimally small the risk, they were there, around each and every corner. It was like she had some kind of magnifying *danger*-periscope.

And now, suddenly, and as a father-to-be, so do I.

'Usual rules apply!' I will yell at my wife, as she embarks upon some unnecessary, life-threatening mission, like popping to the shops to buy milk, or sitting in the garden looking at birds.

'Rule 1: No talking to strangers!'

'Fine!' she will shout back.

'Rule 2: Look both ways when crossing the road!'

'Will do!' she'll reply, casually, as she slides into her winter coat, and I will be concerned she is not listening.

'In fact – no! Look right twice!'

'Yep!'

'Did you hear me? Look right twice! Look right, then left, then right again!'

'Sure thing,' she'll mumble, and then she'll usually mumble something else, but it's almost like she doesn't want me to hear it. It's probably something grateful.

So I'll run downstairs, to make sure she understands.

'You're Australian – we drive on the left over here.'

'I know. I've been here eight years. And also, we drive on the left over *there*.'

'Yes, but you might forget. You're crossing the road for *two* now. I can't always be there to get you across the road. That is an unreasonable demand!'

'I will look left twice.'

'Right! Look *right* twice! Look, do you want me to come with you?'

'No.'

I hope my wife is not going to be a bad mother.

'What's Rule 1 again?' I say, testing her.

'No looking at strangers.'

'No *talking* to strangers!' I say, desperately. 'You can *look* at strangers! In fact, you *should*, in case they're acting shifty!'

'How do I know if they're acting shifty?'

'I don't know! If they've got their hands in their pockets, or they're mumbling, or if they're carrying a knife. Use your mother's intuition.'

'Yes. Because usually I would *approach* strangers carrying knives. Maybe try and *cuddle* them.'

I give her a stern look. One that says, 'Don't be so silly.'

She sighs.

'So I should stare at strangers?'

'No!' I say, my head in my hands. 'Don't *stare* at them! That might aggravate them! Do not aggravate strangers! That can be Rule 3!'

She smiles, and walks towards me, to give me a reassuring hug. 'We'll be OK,' she says, rubbing her tummy.

'Mind your step,' I say, testily.

I stand at the window and watch her walk down the street. It's a bright, crisp day. There's grit on the pavement and no ice to be seen. I made sure she tied her shoelaces properly.

As she disappears around the corner without incident (she is lucky this time), I decide maybe there's the possibility I'm over-thinking things. Maybe this'll calm down, this worrying. Maybe it just does after a while.

I call my mum for a catch-up, and tell her the mother of her future grandchild has just popped to the shops.

There is a sharp intake of breath.

'Why didn't you go *with* her?' she says, appalled, and I feel a little better.

FRANK

The last of the snow is gone and all that is left is the slush on my shoe.

It's still a mercilessly cold day, and the whole city shivers in a chill wind, so I am grateful and thankful and happy to be riding the underground, where the winds are warm and the carriage smells of fried chicken.

I'm heading into town to buy a new printer cartridge and my mind is elsewhere as the tube arrives at Holborn, but as I step off another man steps on and my mind is jolted.

I recognise him. It's Frank!

Frank, from where I used to work!

You know – *Frank*!

'Frank!' I say, turning.

The man turns to face me. He looks testy and like he's in a hurry, but it's Frank all right! Good old Frank! Good old Frank from where I used to work!

'It's Danny!' I say, and he smiles, and says, 'Oh! Yeah! How are *you*?'

And then there's the beep-beep-beep to let us know the doors will be closing any second, and I say, 'I'm good – and *you*?', which is a terrible mistake, because now Frank's faced with a tricky choice: does he just nod and then wave and say goodbye, or does he jump *off* the train and answer me *properly*?

He jumps off the train, squeezing through the doors as they close.

'I'm very well!' he says, the train moving away behind him.

Well, that was nice of him. Now we'll have a little chat before the next one arrives, in …

I look up at the board.

'9 Minutes.'

Nine minutes? Since when do trains take *nine minutes?*

Oh my God, I think. I've delayed him by nine minutes! Now I have to *talk* to him for nine minutes! And not just *talk* to him – *entertain* him!

I smile at Frank.

'So …' I say, in a jaunty voice. 'How have you been?'

'Yes, very … well,' he says, and smiles back.

I kick myself. I had only just asked him how he is, and now I've asked him how he's *been*. What do I ask him next? How he *expects* to be?

Nine minutes! For the love of God, I have to come up with *nine minutes'* worth of stuff! I'm not worth nine minutes! I can't sustain that level of high-octane entertainment! But I *owe* him! I owe Frank!

'And how is your wife?' I try.

'My wife?' he says.

'Or girlfriend!' I say.

I suddenly realise I don't know Frank very well at all. Why had I acted so excited to see him? I'd probably only met him five times before, and *that* was ten years ago, and now I'd inadvertently tricked him into getting off the tube to have a bad conversation.

'She's fine,' he says, but I've already forgotten what I asked him.

I steal a surreptitious glance at the board. It still says 9 Minutes. How can it *still* say 9 Minutes? I mask my exasperation with a smile and I think of something to say. But what can I say that lasts nine minutes? What have I got in my arsenal? And then Frank picks up the slack.

'So where are you on your way to?' he asks.

'Oh!' I say, and I'm pleased, because I *know* this. 'I'm off to buy a new printer cartridge!'

Frank's face falls a little. I search my mind for any funny anecdotes about printer cartridges, but the only ones I've got are too rude.

'Probably from Ryman's,' I say. 'Or another place. My black one has run out. I use that one the most.'

The board now says 8 Minutes. This is good. We're getting somewhere.

'Some of the colour ones run out quickly too,' I add. 'Like the pink one – but that's weird, because I *never* print in pink.'

I take yet another look at the board, but that's mental, because there's no *way* it can be 7 Minutes yet.

'Well, anyway, good to see you,' says Frank, and although I'm relieved because he's clearly winding things up, I'm embarrassed because I'm being dismissed. And not only that – it's implied that Frank would rather have eight minutes on his own than eight minutes with me talking about printer cartridges.

But then something weird happens. He turns and walks off.

Him – not *me*.

He is pretending that he is exactly where he meant to be, even though he knows I know he is supposed to be waiting for the train.

He is saving me the embarrassment of walking off by doing it for me.

But now *I* don't know what to do. He has walked off in the direction *I'm* supposed to be going. And now I *can't* go that way in case I bump into him again.

So I wait seven minutes, and when Frank's train arrives, I wait for the doors to open, and I step on board.

THE WINGMAN

Steve has lost his lucky walnut and is blaming a recent spate of bad luck on this and this alone.

I didn't even know Steve *had* a lucky walnut.

'It was quite a recent thing,' he explains, and then looks glum. 'But now it's gone.'

'But you know life can't work that way,' I reassure him, gently. 'Fortune and misfortune can't be reliant on you carrying a walnut around. People don't get run over because they haven't got a walnut in their pocket.'

'I s'pose,' says Steve, shrugging. 'But it was nice to have around, that walnut. It gave me *confidence*. It was like my wingman.'

'You can't have a walnut as a wingman,' I say.

'Wingmen come in all forms, Dan.'

'Not in *nut* form,' I say, and I say it firmly, because I'm quite sure about this. 'And anyway, *I'm* your wingman!'

He smiles at me, and I smile at him. It is intended to be a nice moment. As it turns out, it is also a mistake.

The next evening, I get a text.

'Wingman! I need you!'

Steve is meeting some girls at our local pub – one of whom he's interested in.

'She's great,' he says, when I call him. 'She's a bit younger than me, but she's American, and she's lovely. You have to be my wingman. You said you would!'

I sense the urgency of the situation and I agree to be his replacement walnut for the evening.

When I get there, Steve is already next to the girl, and things are not going well.

'She's just told me I *smell*!' he whispers.

'Maybe she meant of cupcakes, or something positive,' I whisper, but by whispering I have to get closer to him, and I can tell that she didn't.

The girl, chatting to her friends, gets up to go to the toilet. We can now speak freely.

'It's not my fault!' says Steve. 'I was late and I had to jog here!'

'Calm down,' I say. 'When she gets back, engage her in conversation.'

He looks pleased I am taking my wingman duties seriously.

'Talk about something American,' I suggest.

'Like what?'

'I dunno! Your favourite American celebrity or something.'

The girl sits back down and I listen as Steve follows my quite bad advice.

'You know Michael Keaton?' he says, and she looks at him, unsurely. 'I wonder if he's done any new films lately?'

The girl smiles, but not in what I'd call a good way, and my friend loses his nerve and turns back to me. He has managed to follow quite bad advice quite badly.

'*Michael Keaton* is your favourite American celebrity?' I say. 'Michael Keaton from *Herbie Fully Loaded*? *Mr. Mom* Michael Keaton?'

'He's the only one I could think of! But it's the smell, Dan! I'll never recover from that!'

'Go to the toilets,' I say calmly. 'Use the handwash under your arms!'

'Oh, that's *great* advice, wingman!' he says, and I *think* he was saying it sarcastically. 'Maybe I should wash my feet in the urinals, too. Give me your keys.'

'What?'

'Your place is closer. I'll go there, grab some deodorant, comb my hair and be back in a jiffy.'

I hand him my keys and sit on my own while the American girl laughs with her friends.

Ten minutes later, he's back.

'I couldn't find any deodorant,' he says, sitting down grumpily, and as he does so, I'm hit with a wave of something.

'What have you *done*?' I say, and I pause, because there's something very *familiar* about that smell.

'I used room spray,' he says.

'You used *room spray*?'

'I used room spray.'

I sniff again. He has. He's used room spray. He's used Sainsbury's Grapefruit and Lime *Room Spray*.

'Why would you use *room spray*?' I ask, eyes wide.

'You're not supposed to criticise me as my wingman,' he says. 'You're supposed to nurture and support me! Anyway, I've thought of another celebrity.'

He turns back to the girl and starts talking about Miley Cyrus and there's a wonderful moment where the smell hits her and she tries not to let it show.

'I don't think I'll be requiring your services in the future,' says Steve, as we trudge away from the pub, alone. The girl has gone out clubbing with her friends and did not extend an invite. 'Your advice wasn't the best.'

'*My* advice? *You* talked about Michael Keaton and sprayed yourself with room spray!'

'Still,' he says. 'Would that have happened with the walnut?'

I stubbornly agree that it wouldn't.

In the morning, I put a peanut in an envelope, and send it to him.

THE SHOW

I am in the car park outside the exhibition centre and it is a terrifying sight.

Most of Europe's estate cars and 4X4s seem to have congregated here; miles of sensibly coloured vehicles on each and every side, with hundreds of little yellow warning triangles in the back window.

Which *all* say *Baby on Board*.

My wife thought it would be a good idea to buy two tickets for The Baby Show. I steel myself for whatever's going on in this huge and sinister building.

We trudge alongside other couples, some pregnant, some pushing prams with angry-faced babies inside, and get to the doors.

'Are you sure you want to do this?' says my wife.

'Of course!' I say, because I am an excellent husband. 'There is nothing I want more than to go into The Baby Show.'

We nod at each other, fix looks of grim determination, and enter a world of mayhem and noise.

There are women breastfeeding by the door. A toddler is trying to pull an exhibitor's stand down. Couples wearing matching Teletubbies hats. And smug men with papooses talking loudly.

'It's so hard to look smug with a papoose,' I whisper to my wife. 'Yet these men can do it. How do they know what to do?'

'I guess you just pick it up,' she says, looking as confused as me.

There are hundreds of stands, with thousands of products. Products I've never heard of, from companies I've never needed before. But in here, to these people – the breeders – these companies are *rock and roll*.

Baby Blooms. Baby Oomph. Baby Planet. Babyboomboom. BambooBaby. Bitty Plum. Bum Genius.

I am overwhelmed. I recognise *nothing*. It's like shopping in Aldi.

'Where do we start?' I say. 'What do we need? Why are we here?'

'I just thought it'd be a good stepping stone,' says my wife. 'Maybe start to pick up the essentials …'

But what *are* the essentials? And then …

'A papoose!' I realise. 'I could get a papoose and look smug! And Colin *told* me I'd need a papoose! He said it was *necessary*!'

'Colin thinks *Nando's* is necessary.'

'Oh, and I suppose it *isn't*?' I say, offended.

Sometimes I wonder if my wife will ever understand me.

We start to make our way to a papoose stand, confident now that we finally have a *mission*, and taking in more alien company names.

'Chatterpants,' I say, eyes wide. 'Stinky Whizzers. Look – Future Freak. Who's going to want to raise their baby as a Future Freak?'

I realise I am saying this a little too close to the people at Future Freak, and so we wade deeper into the exhibition. To our right, Lisa Scott-Lee drags her husband past a Dribble Bibs stand. He looks pale and tired. He may have been here some time. Our eyes meet momentarily, and we nod a nod of pained understanding. We will never see each other again, we two men, but already we have exchanged more than we will ever need.

Finally, we make it to the papooses. We stand and stare at the different baby carriers. Take in their different colours. Their different functions. The optional rain covers, sun shades and pillows. There are pamphlets about S-shaped shoulder pads and load-bearing support and three-point adjustable back systems.

We stare blankly.

'Maybe a papoose was setting the bar too high,' I say. 'Maybe we need to build up to this.'

'What's a three-point adjustable back system?' says my wife. 'Are S-shaped shoulder pads good?'

And so slowly, we wander away, like zombies, our eyes glazed over and our confidence sapped. We do not know what to do. I know it and she knows it. We're clueless in a world where everyone else has all the clues.

We leave The Baby Show an hour later. We have bought a blanket and a CD of Radiohead songs re-recorded as lullabies.

I listen to the CD twice in the car on the way home and feel calmer about things.

'We'll get there,' says my wife, as we pull up outside our house. 'Together.'

I give Colin a call. He meets me for a pint, and afterwards, we go for a Nando's.

My wife comes too.

LOVE

There is a story I tell that my wife has heard a thousand times, but the perfect opportunity to tell it has just arisen. It is as if the Gods of Storytelling themselves have somehow manufactured this moment for just this reason, gathering just the right people at just the right time and giving me just the right in.

It's about apple juice.

'Well,' I say, to the people standing around me. I'm already smiling because I know and appreciate how kind the Gods have been today. 'This one time, right, my friend Will got into a scrape involving a bottle of Appletiser ...'

The people around me – four of them – start to smile with anticipation, but I can feel myself losing my wife's attention. No matter. When it comes to anecdotes, there will always be casualties.

'Basically,' I say, 'we were in a hotel just north of Knutsford ...'

My smile grows as I think of what's coming.

'And Will, who's very picky about his drinks, was sure he'd–'

'My *cousin* lives near Knutsford,' interrupts one of the people, and he makes an impressed face, as if to say, 'What a strange coincidence!' I know I have to act fast to cut this line of conversation off. We can afford no diversions on this very special journey.

'Really?' I say, politely. 'Anyway, Will was certain he'd ordered an Appletiser, and I mean *absolutely* certain–'

'Whereabouts near Knutsford?' says someone else.

'Cheadle,' says the first person, brightly.

I pretend I haven't heard.

'So Will thought he'd ordered an Appletiser, but when it came–'

'As in *Don* Cheadle?' says the other guy.

'Yeah, I suppose so!' says the first, and I have to pause while they have a big laugh about it.

'So anyway,' I say, firmly, 'Will thought he was getting an Appletiser–'

'I go past Cheadle sometimes,' says the second person, and I realise the lure of a conversation about Cheadle is just too great for some. I cut my losses, and focus my attention on the remaining two people, who are still with me.

'But when the drink arrived, there was something a bit odd about it–'

'What did you think of Knutsford, Danny? What hotel were you at?'

I turn back to the first person.

'It was nice. A Travelodge, I think.'

'That's a good one, Knutsford,' he says. 'That's a good one, that one.'

'So anyway,' I say, realising I now have to fill him in on what he's missed, 'when the drink arrived, there was something a bit odd about it–'

'I've never been sure about Appletiser,' says one of the others. 'It's a little too fizzy.'

'Sure,' I say, nodding vigorously, trying to show I was taking their opinion on board, but that there were other, more pressing matters than the fizz ratio of carbonated fruit drinks.

'Apple Tango for me,' says the first man, undermining my theory. 'Do they still *do* Apple Tango?'

'Market leader,' I say. 'So Will ordered this Appletiser–'

'What about Um Bungo?' says the second. 'Can you still get that?'

My wife is nearly asleep at this point. I need to move this along.

'So the waiter brings his drink over–'

'What was that jingle Um Bungo had?'

This is turning into *I Love 1983*.

'*Um Bungo Um Bungo They Drink It In The Congo*,' I say, quickly. 'So Will looks at his drink–'

'I used to love that advert,' says the first man.

'Yeah, it was terrific,' says the second.

I decide to drop them again and concentrate on the other two, but they're looking at me with glassy eyes. I'm losing them. I don't know if you've ever tried to talk about Appletiser with people who only want to talk about Um Bungo, but it's really very frustrating.

'So Will looks at his drink, and says, "Did I order this?",' I say, and now I can see the end in sight, and I know my wife must be so pleased this is nearly over. 'And the waiter looks at him …'

I fix my eyes on my tiny audience, who I'm certain are willing me on, fascinated by my tale, and I'm momentarily encouraged, and then one of them says, 'Is Knutsford in Cheshire?', and then the four of them all start talking about Cheshire and Stockport and Wrexham and Crewe, and I stand there, mere inches from the punchline, ready for the big finish, a broken, humiliated man.

And then I feel a hand on my arm, and I turn, and my pregnant wife is looking at me with her big eyes, and she smiles and says, 'Go on …'

And so I tell the whole rest of the story to a woman who's heard it more times than me.

And at the end, she laughs.

And that, my friend, is what love is.

THE WISDOM AND PHILOSOPHIES OF A MODERN MAN: 4

SUNDAY

I'll tell you what *I* like.

I like it when people look at modern art and pompously ask, 'Yes, but is it art?' Therefore I have decided to try and win the Turner Prize, so I can witness it firsthand.

I will place a very smooth and shiny white pebble in a huge room, lit by a single spotlight.

And on the pebble will be a sentence. And this sentence will be written entirely in Braille.

It will say 'Do Not Touch'.

MONDAY

I think the main reason I detest the personalised address book industry is that when you think about it, it's all about who you know.

TUESDAY

Customer service in this country is going from strength to strength.

Last night, a waiter asked me if everything was all right with my dinner.

'It's excellent,' I said. 'Although this wine is a bit runny.'

He looked at my glass.

'I'm so sorry about that, would you like me to replace it?'

I thought about saying yes, but didn't want to cause a fuss, so shut up, and drank my runny wine.

WEDNESDAY

I think if I ever worked for the *Sun*, it would mainly be so I could start describing archaeologists as Coffin Boffins.

THURSDAY

I had a dream last night.

It has made me realise that possibly my favourite dreams have to be the ones where something really crazy and unbelievable happens and then just when it seems it can't get any more crazy or unbelievable, I wake up … and it was *all just a dream*.

Man, I'll never get bored of that twist.

FRIDAY

'It's just so hard starting a charity,' said the posh lady at the bar, wearily, while my wife stood nearby.

'What's the charity?' asked the barman.

'Oh, bears,' she said.

'What type of bears?' he asked.

'Just *bears*,' she said, testily. 'We don't discriminate.'

She cast him a look as if to say he was *just* the sort of man to discriminate against bears.

'Well, good luck,' he said.

'HA!' she said, turning away, as if he could *never* understand what it must be like having no idea what you're doing.

SATURDAY

You know what would be really interesting? If you could teach babies to talk.

Like, not straight away, because they'd have nothing to say and it'd be boring, but later, after a few years, when they got a bit older.

And that, my friends, is all I think about that.

And so, if you'll forgive me, now I must away, and prepare for fatherhood.

DANNY WOULD LIKE TO THANK

Greta Wallace. Ian & Trudy Wallace.

Lisa Thomas for her chance encounter at the Edinburgh Festival and what followed. Phil Hilton, Ross Brown, Terri White, Matt Phare, Matt Hill, Howard Calvert, Jamie Klinger, Mike Soutar, and everyone else at the brilliant *ShortList* magazine.

William Colin Sansom, Wag Colin Marshall-Page, Ian Colin Collins, Dan Steve Vincent, Richard Paul Bacon, Marc Steve Haynes, Rich Steve Fulcher, Richard Rich Glover, Mike Hanson, Graham Linehan, Stefan Gates, Georgia Glyn-Smith, Pete Donaldson, Rebecca Bacon, and everyone else who makes an appearance in this book, whether by real name or not, including Su Pollard and GMTV's Richard Arnold.

Jake Lingwood, Simon Trewin, Jago Irwin, Emily Hickman, Ali Nightingale and Ed Griffiths – thanks.

Tiffany Daniel, Howard Sanders, David Heyman, Lauren Meltzner, Richard Jason Gold, Dan Erlij, Larry Salz, Nancy Gates, David Sussman – thanks to you, too.

Oh.

And, of course, to you.

Bye!

www.dannywallace.com

'Very funny ... so buoyant, and so comically full of faith'
Guardian

'Wildly funny' *Daily Mail*

'One of those rare books that actually has the potential
to change your life...' *San Francisco Bay Guardian*

'Hilarious' *Heat*

Yes Man is the story of what happened when Danny decided
to say Yes to everything, in order to make his life a little
more interesting. And boy... did it get more interesting...

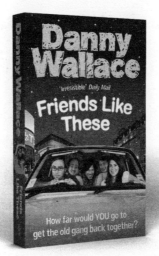

'Irresistible' *Daily Mail*

'The funniest book you'll read this year' *ShortList*

'The poster-boy for positive thinking' *Guardian*

'Hilarious and genuinely touching' *Heat*

Danny Wallace sets off on a brand new quest: to find his childhood friends and see how they're dealing with being grown-up too...

Danny Wallace titles are also available on audio!

Perfect for commuting, travel or for when you fancy sitting back and listening to one of Danny's rip-roaringly funny tales – read by the man himself.

Awkward Situations for Men is available to download from iTunes and www.audible.co.uk in four hilarious episodes.

Also available: